Working with Violence

Edited by

Carol Lupton and Terry Gillespie

Foreword by Jalna Hanmer

MACMILLAN

First published 1994 by
MACMILLAN PRESS LTD
Houndmills, Basingstoke, Hampshire RG21 2XS
and London
Companies and representatives
throughout the world

ISBN 0–333–56743–9 hardcover
ISBN 0–333–56744–7 paperback

A catalogue record for this book is available
from the British Library.

10 9 8 7 6 5 4 3 2 1
03 02 01 00 99 98 97 96 95

Printed in China

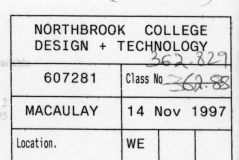

Series Standing Order (Practical Social Work)

If you would like to receive future titles in this series as they are published, you can make
use of our standing order facility. To place a standing order please contact your
bookseller or, in case of difficulty, write to us at the address below with your name and
address and the name of the series. Please state with which title you wish to begin your
standing order. (If you live outside the United Kingdom we may not have the rights for
your area, in which case we will forward your order to the publisher concerned.)

Customer Services Department, Macmillan Distribution Ltd
Houndmills, Basingstoke, Hampshire RG21 2XS, England

For Mark, Daniel, Jack and Tess (*Carol Lupton*)

For my daughter Jane, and my mother Jane
(*Terry Gillespie*)

Contents

Foreword

During the past twenty years women have raised the issue of violence by men against women – and, more, often than not, this is committed by men already known to the women concerned. Women-centred practices have developed, but the existence of agencies that listen to women and base their professional practice on women's needs remains a partially achieved goal. Why this is so is a crucial question.

The knowledge, understanding and responses of women's agencies have yet to be fully accepted and integrated into statutory services, although there are individual women in the full range of agencies with a woman-centred or feminist approach to their work. Working with violence in ways that are sensitive to the subjectivity of women not only means acknowledging the forms it can take – emotional, sexual and physical – but also acknowledging how different social locations can affect both experiences of violence and responses to it. This book addresses both commonalities and differences in women's experiences of violence and the professional practices that are needed to respond appropriately to women and to men.

The full complexity of the problem is exposed by drawing together experiences of providing services in both the voluntary and statutory sectors with experiences of women service users and professional staff. A focus on the interrelationship of theories, policies and practices demonstrates how institutional issues adversely affect the quality of professional intervention. Theory is a major site of struggle for professional and institutional dominance.

By focusing on specific professional groups, an understanding of what is wrong, what needs to change, and how this can be achieved, can be addressed. This book is to be warmly welcomed as it explores how to develop a more responsive, and responsible, social welfare practice for women.

JALNER HANMER
Reader in Women's Studies and
Co-Convenor of the Research Unit
on Violence, Abuse and Gender
Relations, University of Bradford

Acknowledgements

To the members of the British Sociological Association Violence Against Women Study Group who provided a source of scholarly inspiration and support; to Susie Waller and Diana Warren-Holland who were key contributors to the early planning stages of the book; to Sophie Evans of the Social Services Research and Information Unit at the University of Portsmouth for help in typing the transcripts; to Jo Campling and Frances Arnold at Macmillan for their support and encouragement throughout the project, and to Jalna Hanmer for her advice and guidance. In addition we acknowledge the contributions of women in Rape Crisis Centres, Women's Aid Refuges and other organisations, within both statutory and voluntary sectors, who are working on a daily basis with, and struggling to improve services in, the area of violence against women and children.

CAROL LUPTON
TERRY GILLESPIE

List of Abbreviations

ACOP	Association of Chief Officers of Probation
BASW	British Association of Social Work
CCETSW	Central Council for the Education and Training of Social Workers
CHC	Community Health Council
CPS	Crown Prosecution Service
LRCC	London Rape Crisis Centre
NAPO	National Association of Probation Officers
NAVSS	National Association of Victim Support Schemes
NCVO	National Council for Voluntary Organisations
NPRIE	National Probation Research and Information Centre
NSPCC	National Society for the Prevention of Cruelty to Children
PICA	Public Interest Case Assessment Schemes
POW	Prostitute Outreach Workers
RCC	Rape Crisis Centre
RTS	Rape Trauma Syndrome
SARC	Sexual Assault Referral Centre
SSD	Social Services Department
VSS	Victim Support Scheme
WAFE	Womens Aid Federation England
WAR	Women Against Rape
WAVAW	Women Against Violence Against Women

Introduction

Background

This book addresses the practical problems and possibilities of 'doing feminism' in the 1990s. The chapters identify and critically examine the dilemmas for feminist theory and practice, while at the same time taking stock of feminist responses to varieties of men's violence. They outline a range of strategies employed by feminist service providers working in the field of violence against women in a number of statutory and non-statutory agencies. The contributors all have practical experience of working with the reality of violence perpetrated by men. While as individuals they are personally and intellectually committed to a range of different feminist theoretical positions, they all share the common difficulty of making connections between those theories and their everyday personal and professional lives. In particular, many experience the problem of reconciling their personal oppression within masculinist organisational structures with the power that they, as part of those organisations, may wield over the lives of other women. A central concern of the text derives from the awareness of those contributing that they may, through their work, at times serve to compound or heighten the specific oppression suffered by many women and girls.

Feminist theories and campaigning work, including working in the areas of violence against women and children, have been charted historically: 'first and second waves' of feminism have been identified, with the latter located at the start of the 1970s (Edwards, 1987). It was in the early 1970s that feminists both in the USA and in Britain collectively explored and articulated shared experiences of violence and sexual abuse, setting up the first rape crisis lines and refuges for battered women (Kelly, 1988). Many feminists argued that violence against women is endemic in a patriarchal society where men as a group or social class have control over women in both public and private spheres. This is the case whether or not individual men choose to sexually abuse or do violence to women and children (Brownmiller, 1976; Stanko, 1985; Kelly, 1988).

There is, however, no single feminist standpoint on this or any other issue. As the individual chapters in this book reflect, feminism embodies a range of different theoretical and political perspectives. Attempts to categorise different 'feminisms' have typically identified liberal, radical, socialist/ Marxist and black feminist variants (Lovell, 1990; Humm, 1992; Tong, 1989). More recently, however, feminists have resisted attempts to categorise and define feminism. As Maynard has argued, there are major problems with the assignation of feminists to particular categories: 'For one thing, the categories selected tend to be far from homogeneous, often containing writers with different emphases. For another, not every feminist fits into the kinds of classification which are usually constructed' (1993: 120).

Whichever theoretical variant of feminism one adopts, a basic premise is the general oppression of women by men. While we must acknowledge the complex nature of this oppression in any specific context, its cutting edge, its most direct and physical manifestation, is men's violence against women and children. Although it should be recognised that women may be oppressed by other women and may share aspects of their oppression with men, nevertheless where violence against women and children is concerned, it occurs largely at the hands of men. Nevertheless, it is important to acknowledge that women's experiences of, and responses to, men's violence are differentiated along lines of race, ethnicity, class, age, sexuality and physical ability. Women from black, Asian and minority ethnic communities have documented their experiences of violence and abuse, emphasising the particular difficulties for women when violence is perpetrated by men from within their communities (Bryan, Dadzie and Scafe, 1985; Mama, 1989b; see also Chapters 4 and 5 in this volume). Mama, who uses the term 'black women' to refer to women from African, Asian and Caribbean backgrounds, argues that black women struggle alongside black men against the racism endemic in British society. Hence the wariness of black women when approaching statutory agencies for help and support in escaping male violence, for fear that state intervention may excacerbate racism. For Mama:

> In the case of black women, male violence in the home is compounded by general societal racism and state repression, to create a situation of multiple oppression and further punishment for those bravely struggling to establish lives for themselves and their children, away from violent men (1989b: xiii).

Feminism in a cold climate

The 1980s have changed dramatically the wider socio-political context of feminist practice. Three central aspects of these changes are of particular relevance to a text about the service response to men's violence. The first is the restructuring of publicly provided health and social care provision that culminated in the 1990 NHS and Community Care Act. Key related features of this process – the pressure to achieve greater efficiency and economy, the stimulation of a 'mixed economy of care' with an enhanced role for the voluntary and independent sector, the growth of internal markets and the 'purchaser/provider' divide – have had profound implications for the way in which both statutory and non-statutory agencies organise and deliver their services. The second major area of change has resulted from the keen determination of central government to exert greater financial and political control over key areas of public expenditure, particularly that of local authorities. Increased constraints over local government spending have served to reduce the funding and resources available to both statutory and non-statutory service providers at a local level. With the exception of the mental health specific grant, for example, the planned expansion of community-based care has not been underpinned by any additional 'ring-fenced' funding. In particular, the explicit political encouragement given to the voluntary and independent sector has not afforded it any greater degree of financial security. The last, and possibly the most crucial, area of change has been ideological in nature. The whole policy thrust of the 'Thatcher years' has sought to redress the balance of responsibility between the individual and the state and between deserving and non-deserving categories of 'citizen'. In a series of legislative changes, emphasis has been placed on the importance of self-help and self-reliance and on individual rather than collective solutions to social problems. Central to this policy shift has been the attempt to reassert the moral and social centrality of the family unit.

Surviving the backlash

Stimulated by, and in turn underpinning, this ideological shift has been the emergence of a multi-faceted backlash against the theory and practice of feminism. This backlash gathered momentum in the early 1990s with the representation in the media of an anti-feminist discourse uniting such diverse groups as the moral right, 'post-feminists', men's groups and liberal commentators who have expressed an often barely concealed (and at times outright) animosity towards feminist theory and practice (Rush, 1990; Faludi, 1992). This moral panic has been reflected in public debates about the influence of feminism on mainstream culture, while 'malestream' academics have anguished about the proliferation of women's studies courses in US and British universities.

It is clear, however that, despite the increasingly 'cold climate' of the 1980s, feminists have achieved a good deal of success in terms of heightening public awareness, and subsequently shaping support services, for women and children in the context of men's violence. We should not lose sight of the fact that policy-makers in the fields of health and social services, housing, the police and the criminal justice system more generally have responded, to greater or lesser degrees, to the demands made by feminists for better provision of services. This has included the provision of funding for refuges, Rape Crisis Centres, counselling and crisis lines, and for the establishment of 'domestic violence units' and victim examination suites (see Chapters 1, 2 and 3 in this volume for feminist critiques of these 'new initiatives').

Nevertheless, we cannot afford to be complacent about the extent of these evident successes. Where services have improved, it has been as a result of hard-won struggles by feminists working within a context of financial and other resource constraints. These struggles are variously documented in the chapters of this book. Feminists working in both the statutory and voluntary sectors have had to work hard to negotiate and win resources and this has often necessitated new ways of working. It has, for example, typically involved devising strategies of resistance to state incorporation of essentially feminist, women-centred modes of organisation. Many autonomous women's groups have had to perform a delicate balancing act between maintaining a commitment to feminist theory and practice, while working closely with the more traditional mainstream agencies who provide funding and facilitate service provision.

A particular tension between feminist groups and these agencies has developed around the use of terminology. For example, feminists working in the frontline of violence against women have been critical of agencies, particularly those within or working closely with the criminal justice system, who refer to women who have experienced sexual and physical violence as 'victims'. Stanko and others have highlighted the problematic nature of this term, arguing that victim typologies objectify and minimise women's experiences of men's violence (Stanko, 1985; see also Chapters 1 and 2 in this volume). Categories such as 'victim precipitation' and 'victim provocation' have served to underpin and justify the often unfair treatment of abused women and children by criminal justice

agencies and society more generally. The notion of women as
victims separates women who have experienced sexual and
physical violence from other women and therefore seeks to
deny the commonality of women's shared experiences of
violence and abuse. Women working in the field of violence
against women, including women who have themselves
suffered such violence, often prefer to use the term 'survivor'
as this encapsulates women's capacities to survive abuse.
Survivors of violence were instrumental in setting up Rape
Crisis Centres, refuges for battered women, incest survivor
groups and other support services for women and children.
The term 'survivor' thus empowers women who have
historically resisted and campaigned against men's violence
against women and children (Stanko, 1985).

We have in this book referred to women as survivors of
violence, while acknowledging the use of the term 'victim' in
the context of women's treatment within the criminal justice
system and by other agencies who impose categories on
women's experiences of violence. In the same way we have
used the term 'wife assault' in our discussions about violence
against women by men within the home. While we acknowledge that such violence is often perpetrated by males with
whom women are living but to whom they are not married,
retention of the term 'wife' serves to indicate the fact that this
violence occurs in a marriage-like situation. This establishes a
strong contrast with the notion of home as a place of safety in
an otherwise dangerous world. The widespread use of the
gender-neutral term of 'domestic abuse' by more mainstream
service providers is eschewed in so far as it serves to obscure
the fact that, in the great majority of cases, we are dealing with
violence that is inflicted by men on women.

Feminism in practice

The first three chapters of this book examine some of the more
general tendencies affecting the work of those attempting to

develop feminist practice. Each focuses on the work of autonomous women's groups and explores their operation in the context of other statutory and non-statutory service providers. Chapters 1 and 2 examine the organisation and strategies of resistance developed by Rape Crisis Centres (RCCs).

In Chapter 1 Terry Gillespie focuses on the relationship of the Centres to the police and Victim Support Schemes (VSS). She describes how RCCs in Britain have largely survived the difficulties encountered by most voluntary and independent agencies during the 1980s. They have provided effective, specifically feminist needs-based services for women and girls who have suffered men's sexual violence. The majority of RCCs in Britain, unlike their counterparts in the USA, continue to operate as autonomous, or 'relatively autonomous' (Brenton, 1985) women's groups committed to providing confidential, women-centred support and counselling services. RCCs are acknowledged by statutory and voluntary agencies alike as the frontline providers of specialist knowledge and expertise in the field of support services for rape survivors.

Gillespie documents the pressures experienced by RCCs in the face of attempts to discredit the work of autonomous women's groups more generally. She charts how they have worked with the consequent threat of marginalisation or loss of funding, particularly with the emergence of alternative support services, most notably VSS, during the 1980s. Such pressures have been widely resisted through a variety of strategies and initiatives, outlined in Chapter 1, to ensure the continuation of the provision of quality services for women by women.

In Chapter 2 Marian Foley looks more widely at the tendencies towards the professionalisation and medicalisation of the response to rape. These tendencies, she argues, are encapsulated in the emergence in Britain of the first Sexual Assault Referral Centre (SARC) staffed by nurses, psychosexual counsellors and working in close collaboration with the local police. The Centre has been seen as a prototype of statutory service provision for 'victims' of rape and sexual assault and has attracted much interest from the police. Foley argues that the SARC seeks to individualise and depoliticise the issue of rape and men's violence by placing it within a 'medical' context. This has the effect of marginalising the expertise of Rape Crisis Centres whose policies and practice are seen as extreme. The development of SARC thus raises the central question, faced by many autonomous women's organisations, of how far they are prepared to compromise their distinctive service philosophy in order to gain wider credibility and financial security. Chapter 2 suggests practical strategies for managing the dilemmas posed by the SARC and by the tendencies towards the professionalisation and medicalisation of rape more generally.

In Chapter 3 Carol Lupton compares the experience of the battered women's refuge movement in the UK with that of its counterpart in the USA. While both initially derived from the concerns and campaigns of the early feminist movement, there is evidence that the US shelters have increasingly begun to adopt more traditional service-provision approaches. Many have abandoned their commitment to non-hierarchical and collectivist modes of organisation and to empowerment and self-help philosophies. There has been a general redefinition of the problem away from that of men's violence against women to an issue of personal or family dysfunction. Lupton examines the extent to which the UK refuge movement is facing similar pressures for change. She argues that such pressures exist, but that refuge groups have developed a number of ways of resisting and negotiating their impact. Nevertheless, in an increasingly hostile political and financial climate, there may be a need for the development of new strategies on the part of those working within the movement.

Chapters 4 to 7 focus more directly on the experience of those suffering from, or working with, men's violence. In Chapter 4 Kish Bhatti-Sinclair examines the problem of wife assault within Britain's Asian communities. She argues that in this area, as in many others, the particular experiences of black and Asian women have been excluded from feminist accounts of the problem. Her chapter sets out to redress the balance by re-presenting, in their own words, the experience of Asian women who have been abused by their husbands. These accounts reveal the interwoven nature of the race and gender oppression suffered by Asian women and the inadequate and ethnocentric nature of the response from a range of service agencies. At times, those turning to Women's Aid refuges for help have also experienced racism and services unresponsive to their religious and cultural needs. As a result, Bhatti-Sinclair argues there is a need for more black and Asian women's refuges. This, however, does not mean that white women can abrogate their responsibility for the needs of battered women from black communities; those working within refuges must critically examine their practice if Asian women are to play a full and equal part in the wider refuge movement.

Chapter 5 examines the keen dilemmas and tensions experienced by those attempting to develop feminist practice in the area of child sexual abuse. Claudia Bernard's critique of the 'family dysfunction' approach still dominant within social work practice reveals the ways in which it ignores the central issue of power relations within the family and can result in a victim-blaming practice. Based on interviews with experienced practitioners, and illustrated by case studies, Bernard's chapter describes the various forms of organisational resistance to those attempting to challenge this dominant approach. In a professional culture that defines itself as objective and value-free, those committed to an anti-oppressive approach will face accusations of 'over-identification' or 'taking sides'. Bernard reveals the extent to which this stance of objectivity is, in a context structured by gender and race oppression, itself inherently value-laden. Like Bhatti-Sinclair, Bernard explores the complex interrelationship of race and gender oppression. She describes how uncertainty about race issues can problematise the response to gender oppression; at the same time, attempts to work in a non-sexist way may fail to take account of the realities of racism in the lives of women and girls. Bernard concedes that the development of good anti-discriminatory practice is difficult, but argues that, despite all the obstacles, there are many practitioners actively committed to the attempt.

Chapter 6 explores the dilemmas for feminists working with prostitute women. Maggie O'Neill argues that feminists need to find ways of supporting and empowering women sex workers and has sought to do this in her research and work with prostitutes. An important aspect of this work has been the development of women-centred practice through the setting up of a multi-agency forum in order to improve service provision to prostitute women. Central to such an initiative, she argues, must be the prioritising and focusing on the self-defined needs of prostitutes who daily encounter the threat and reality of male violence, and yet are marginalised or ignored in terms of statutory support services. For O'Neill, feminists working with prostitute women need to contextualise their experiences within the concept of feminist praxis (Stanley, 1990). This means creating the spaces for prostitute women's voices to be heard while locating their experiences within a clear understanding of the role and power of the masculinist state. To this end, O'Neill calls for feminists to 'join forces in support of women working in the sex industry specifically in relation to interrelated inequalities in the spheres of violence, sexuality, work and power'.

In Chapter 7 Stella Perrott focuses on the work of the probation service with men who abuse women and children. She explores the difficulties faced by women officers working within a male-dominated criminal justice system. Work with male abusers is in itself a major source of tension for many women who may feel that this is a male problem that should be resolved by men. The dominance of androcentric assumptions about women's behaviour and role within the family can result in a degree of collusion between probation officers and male offenders. The commitment of the service to diversion both from custody and prosecution can serve to minimise the seriousness of child and woman abuse. Like Bernard, Perrott explores the absence of support for staff who become anxious or distressed by their work, and highlights the lack of encouragement, indeed at times hostility, often displayed towards those attempting to develop an anti-sexist and anti-racist practice. She too concludes more positively by charting the specific practical ways in which such officers can work together to develop a more campaigning role within the service.

Chapters 8 and 9 take a slightly different look at the issue of working with violence. Chapter 8 examines the issue of violence against social services staff. As Marianne Hester argues, feminists have spent a lot of time examining violence against those without power, yet feminist analysis must also provide an understanding of violence against those with power, particularly if this violence is gender related. Hester examines a number of empirical studies that have been made of social workers' experience of violence and argues that they have largely ignored the issue of gender. Their conclusions have generally been that male staff are more likely to experience violence from service-users than are women staff. The definitions of 'violence' used within these studies, however, have been biased towards the male experience, and methods of data collection have served to underrepresent the experience of women. In particular, Hester argues methodologies have failed to differentiate within the wide-ranging category of 'violence' or to acknowledge the greater tendency of women staff to deny or minimise its occurrence. More gender-sensitive methods developed in subsequent studies and by Hester herself reveal that while male staff are more likely to experience physical violence, women staff face more sexual and/or verbal abuse. Women staff, however, are much less likely than men to talk about the violence they experience or to have that experience acknowledged or validated by their colleagues. Social service authorities need to develop better training and support systems, Hester concludes, if the organisational response to violence against its staff is to be improved.

In Chapter 9 Joan Orme explores the difficult phenomenon of women who are themselves violent. Such women, she argues, pose dilemmas for traditional and feminist theoretical approaches alike to the extent that they challenge essentialist explanations of women's nature as more caring, nurturing and less aggressive than that of men. Orme examines the way in which such assumptions underpin the service response to violent women. In contrast to the 'normality' of male aggression, that of the female is perceived as being 'unnatural' or 'bad'. Explanations for this unnatural behaviour are sought from the female physiology – the behaviour of the 'hysterical body' (de Beauvoir, 1972) – or from a woman's individual psychology. Such medicalisation and pathologisation of women's violence, however, effectively denies the possibility of its rational basis and robs it of any social or cultural meaning. Moreover, this 'sick' model of violent women's behaviour results in their differential treatment. In comparison with their male counterparts, violent women are more likely to be perceived as dangerous and disturbed and to be subject to the intervention of the medical and mental health professions. Orme argues that it is necessary to accept that both male aggression and female passivity are socially constructed; this not only denies the 'abnormality' of female aggression, but allows for the possibility that men can be socialised into non-violent ways.

Across these individual chapters there is inevitably a differential emphasis on the themes of policy, professional practice, research and theory. Nevertheless, they all in their different ways reveal the need for a critical interrelationship between feminist theory and practice. Ultimately, theory is only useful to the extent that it helps us to make sense of real situations and, given the wider feminist project, helps us to change those situations. In turn, our theoretical analyses need to be sharpened and refined through their application to specific contexts. It is important that the development of feminist social theory as an intellectual activity is informed and underpinned by the practical experiences of specific political struggles. This is not to argue that social theories can in this way be reduced to individual or group experiences, as there is no way of making sense of such experiences without a wider understanding of the common threads and underlying tendencies by which they are linked and made explicable. Rather, it is to argue that the progressive evolution of good theory requires that it is constantly held accountable to the realities of women's lives. The aim of this book is to contribute to the development of more effective strategies for feminists working in a range of organisational settings, as well as to inform and extend the broader analyses contained in feminist theoretical work. It is our intention that this book while addressing critically the theoretical and practical difficulties faced by feminists working with violence, should nevertheless seek to empower those women working at the frontline as service provides.

1

Under Pressure: Rape Crisis Centres, Multi-Agency Work and Strategies for Survival

Terry Gillespie

Introduction

This chapter explores the organisational dilemmas, challenges and difficulties facing women working in Rape Crisis Centres (RCCs) in Britain in the 1990s. To this end, I propose to review critically the organisational settings and interface between RCCs on the one hand, as the acknowledged service providers of specialist support services for female survivors of men's violence, and, on the other hand, the police and Victim Support Schemes (VSS), which, respectively, provide statutory and traditional voluntary services for crime victims. My interest in this interface has emerged out of ongoing research[1] into services for survivors[2] of sexual violence.

Informed by this research, the chapter explores a range of issues critical to the survival and development of RCCs. For example, how have RCCs responded to the general funding crisis for voluntary groups in Britain? Is it the case that autonomous women's groups, following the North American model (O'Sullivan, 1978; Schechter, 1982), have been gradually incorporated into the state through financial and political pressures? Have RCCs been marginalised by the growth of VSS which have moved slowly but inexorably into the area of service provision for survivors of rape and sexual assault? How do these agencies differ in terms of service

15

philosophy, training and provision for rape survivors? What are the ways forward for RCCs as feminist organisations committed to the enhancement of specialist service provision for female survivors of men's sexual violence? I will explore these issues more fully in the remainder of this chapter.

The history and development of RCCs

RCCs developed out of the resurgence of the women's movement in the 1960s and 1970s in Britain and the USA. Centres, or Rape Crisis Lines as they were more usually known then, were set up in response to a perceived lack of statutory or voluntary provision for female survivors of sexual violence (Kelly, 1988). The first RCC in Britain was established in London in 1976, offering a twenty-four hour telephone counselling service run 'by and for women' (London Rape Crisis Centre, 1984). By 1989 there were at least fifty-five RCCs in England and Wales offering support services to women and girls who have been raped or sexually abused; the majority of these RCCs reported being overstretched, under-resourced and facing an increasing demand for their services.[3]

RCCs tend to operate within an identified feminist model of service provision, adopting a woman-centred practice that seeks to empower women who have been raped or sexually abused (London Rape Crisis Centre, 1984; Stanko, 1985; Mawby and Gill, 1987; Kelly, 1988). They have for the most part attempted to reject 'malestream' organisational modes, preferring to work collectively, non-hierarchically, by sharing skills, and with a commitment to providing effective woman-centred, anti-racist support services for survivors of sexual violence. From their inception British RCCs have sought to operate independently and autonomously from local government, while at the same time seeking funding from local statutory services. It is important to acknowledge the uneven development of RCCs. My national survey of RCCs in England and Wales indicates that they are not homogeneous organisations. Rather, there is no single organisational model identified, although most RCCs identify themselves as specifically 'feminist RCCs'. The variety of organisational modes has developed partly as an outcome of their autonomy and partly through the absence, until relatively recently, of any federal structure. These issues are discussed more fully below.

Typically, RCCs offer practical advice, support and counselling services 'for women, by women', including telephone counselling lines, face-to-face counselling and groupwork where appropriate and where resources allow. Practical help includes the provision of information and advice on medical issues, reporting to the police and court procedures, as well as accompanying and supporting women in their contacts with these agencies. All RCCs provide long-term, needs-based, non-directive and non-judgmental counselling support and offer a totally confidential service. The feminist counselling model seeks to empower women by listening to and believing their accounts of sexual violence, acknowledging that women respond in different ways to experiences of violence, and enabling them to regain control of their lives with the help of long-term support if needed.

The challenges and difficulties encountered by autonomous women's groups in the course of striving to work within an identified feminist framework have been well documented (Hanmer and Maynard, 1987; Hanmer, Radford and Stanko, 1989; Dunhill, 1989; Kelly, 1988; Mama, 1989b; Dobash and Dobash, 1992). Such difficulties, although clearly located within different organisational contexts, can be as acute for feminists working both in the traditional voluntary sector and in statutory agencies. In the course of my research it has become clear that there are women who identify themselves as feminists working within both the police force and VSS who struggle to incorporate a woman-centred approach into their work with women clients (see also Maguire, 1988). Feminists working in a range of organisational settings have campaigned long and hard for agencies to provide more sensitive, needs-based services for women and girls who have suffered violence from men, and welcome genuine improvements in policy and practice. Nevertheless, RCCs have encountered difficulties in their working relationships with statutory organisations, the local police being the most frequently cited, presenting difficulties for effective multi-agency working. However, it needs to be stated that several RCCs report good working relationships with local police officers, while acknowledging that such relationships are somewhat tenuous, need fostering, and are inevitably transient in nature. In their work with statutory agencies, on whom they are frequently dependent for funding, RCCs often experience a disjunction between, on the one hand, their commitment to feminist principles and, on the other, the dilemmas and compromises experienced in practice. While subscribing to a collectively organised, woman-centred approach, nevertheless the conflicts engendered in the context of working on a daily basis in the area of violence against women with agencies who do not, on the whole, share or endorse such an approach, can lead at times to intense frustration. Indeed, traditional voluntary organisations such as VSS and statutory agencies such as the police may well see feminist service provision as being at odds with the goals of 'efficient and effective' service delivery (Maguire and Pointing, 1988; Mawby and Gill, 1987; Gill and Mawby, 1990; Rock, 1990).

Multi-agency working: rhetoric or reality?

Many RCCs experience pressures to compromise organisational principles in the short-term in the context of developing longer-term goals of improved service provision for survivors of rape and sexual abuse. These pressures may be exacerbated in the context both of a funding crisis for voluntary groups in general and the constant threat of marginalisation of autonomous women's groups in particular.

Debunking myths and stereotypes

In the course of my research into RCCs and their relationships with the police and VSS, it has become clear, both from the available literature and in the views expressed by some police officers and VSS volunteers, that myths and stereotypes abound concerning the nature and organisation of centres, about rape, rapists and the 'typical rape victim'.

RCCs have been widely identified in criminological and victim support literature as 'extreme' feminist organisations, anti-police, anti-men and more concerned with 'radical feminist politics' than providing effective support services for women who have been raped and sexually abused (Blair, 1985; Corbett and Hobdell, 1988; Mawby and Gill, 1987; Gill and Mawby, 1990). This is a misrepresentation of RCCs based not on any systematic evidence, but rather on commonly held misconceptions about autonomous women's groups[4]. Such stereotypical views can have implications for the further marginalisation of RCCs by those groups that seek to develop and expand mainstream support services for crime victims. It is indeed the case that most RCCs work within a feminist perspective in their analysis of the causes and effects of sexual violence. A great deal of their work is concerned with educating the wider public, including statutory and voluntary agencies who frequently consult with and request training from RCCs, to challenge the myths and stereotypes around rape, rape 'victims' and typologies of 'the rapist'. An example of such stereotypes can be found in the view expressed by Mawby and Gill that RCC volunteers in North America, predominantly young women students and professionals, 'were thus in some respects scarcely representative of the typical rape victim' (1987: 82). This stereotypical view of women who have been raped is challenged by feminist writers who strongly reject the notion of a 'typical rape victim' arguing that any woman can be a 'victim' of sexual violence regardless of age, race, social or occupational class position (Toner, 1982; Hanmer and Saunders, 1984; London Rape Crisis Centre,

1984; Stanko, 1985; Kelly, 1988; see also the Introduction in this volume). Further, my study found that the majority of RCCs, while primarily offering support services for women and girls, nevertheless accept calls from men, referring those whose partners or relatives have been raped, together with males who themselves have been sexually assaulted, to appropriate support services and survivor groups.

RCC workers spend a good deal of their time in educative or consultative work with local community groups and organisations, while also providing information and training programmes for voluntary and statutory agencies. The training of RCC volunteers tends to be both extensive and ongoing covering specific areas of service provision. During the training period (generally initial training programmes last from six to twelve weeks) volunteers who are considered unsuitable for working within such a specialist support service are usually screened out, with sympathetic referral to support services where appropriate, in the selection procedures adopted almost universally by RCCs. It would be considered inappropriate and potentially damaging if, for example, an RCC counsellor expressed anger or projected her own feelings about men's sexual violence on to a woman who had been raped. Few centres operate an 'open door' policy in recognition of the skills and expertise needed to provide such specialist support services. RCCs typically run a regular volunteer support group where any anger or frustration felt about the perpetrators of rape and sexual abuse can be appropriately expressed and managed. Such support or 'supervision' is necessary in the context of working in such intensive, stressful and sensitive areas; it also helps to alleviate the problem of volunteer 'burnout', while at the same time strengthening group solidarity and commitment.

Managerialism, professionalism, and their impact on RCCs

In the context of the general funding crisis for all voluntary groups in the 1990s, together with the particular ideological backlash against feminist theory and practice (see the Introduction, in this volume), RCCs as feminist frontline grassroots organisations are facing particular challenges. Consequently, they are developing practical strategies for the continued provision of expert and comprehensive support services for rape survivors.

Throughout the 1980s and into the 1990s RCCs have struggled to maintain and develop existing services within the climate of uncertainty arising out of changes in state-funding mechanisms (see also Chapter 3 in this volume). These financial pressures, together with requirements on voluntary agencies generally to provide 'efficient and effective' services, can appear as further evidence of the backlash working against autonomous women's groups (Maguire, 1988).

The pressures towards efficiency and effectiveness in organisation and service delivery can be traced to the rise of 'the new discourse of managerialism' in the public sector (Clarke and Newman, 1992). This discourse places particular pressures on voluntary organisations to conform to corporate management-style policies and practices expressed in the language of internal markets: total quality management, partnership and multi-agency working. The difficulties of 'inter-agency co-operation' have been identified in, for example, the area of situational crime prevention, where it is acknowledged that '. . . in any liaison or collaborative efforts the different agencies do not start on equal terms. Some, so to speak, are more interconnected than others' (Blagg *et al.*, 1988: 216). Again, the enthusiasm of statutory agencies, including the police, for multi-agency working '. . . often remains at the level of rhetoric or sloganising, so that its importance may be symbolic or ideological, rather than indicating much about what is feasible' (Blagg *et al.*, 1988: 216).

Similarly there has been identified an intensification of pressure on Women's Aid refuges and RCCs to professionalise services or risk further marginalisation in the competition for funding sources from local government and statutory agencies (Kelly, 1989a; see also Chapters 2 and 3 in this volume). It is clear from my research to date that RCCs are indeed experiencing some pressure to adopt a 'professional' ethos, with many centres describing themselves as offering 'expert' or 'professional' support services. Indeed, it has been argued that autonomous women's groups need to redefine what it means to be 'professional' (Kelly, 1989a). It is possible to assume the more positive attributes associated with professionalism – for example, established expertise, specialist service provision, consultative work, extensive and ongoing training – while rejecting the more negative aspects commonly identified, such as authoritarianism, male-dominated hierarchies, power structures, 'masculinist' service philosophies and provision implicit in, for example, the medicalisation and pathologisation of rape.

The pressures facing RCCs in their relationships with funding bodies and other statutory and voluntary agencies can be seen as part of the increasing blurring of boundaries between public and voluntary sectors in the 'mixed economy of welfare'. The organisational modes associated with RCCs, including cooperative working, woman-centredness, skills sharing and autonomy, can be seen as out of step with what is happening elsewhere in the interface between voluntary and statutory agencies. Interviews with RCC workers indicate that there is a range of responses to these pressures. While RCCs may have some autonomy from local statutory bodies, nevertheless, like all voluntary service providers, they are experiencing these pressures towards cooptation or incorporation into what can loosely be termed the 'local state'. Such pressures have implications for the management of service funding, for the selection and recruitment of paid workers, and the centralisation of service provision. Indeed some RCCs have responded by adopting a more 'managerialist' approach in the attempt to secure funding and develop service provision.[5] However, many RCCs continue to resist such pressures, adopting a variety of strategies for survival. These are discussed in more detail below.

Funding and the duplication of services

The funding crisis for RCCs necessarily has to be examined in the context of competition with groups seeking to duplicate RCC work. This duplication of services includes statutory services initiatives such as the development of multi-disciplinary centres (typically health, social services and police) for victims of rape and sexual assault along the lines of the North American model (Schechter, 1982; Mawby and Gill, 1987; see also Chapter 2 in this volume).

Within the voluntary sector, 'male rape' survivor groups and support services have recently emerged in Britain. While services are not necessarily being duplicated in the case of male groups, they are nevertheless potential competitors in bids for funding sources and fears have been expressed by RCC workers that funding may be diverted to such groups. Furthermore, some centres have reported pressure, both from statutory agencies and from men who have experienced male sexual violence, to extend support services to men using RCC facilities and resources. There are clearly parallels here with the anxieties expressed by feminist refuge workers over calls for the funding of male refuges (see Chapter 3 in this volume). However, it appears from the research that so far RCCs in Britain have not lost funding to male groups, while a few have responded to these demands by developing and managing separate support services for men (in one case, employing male counsellors) with services either located away from centres used by women or with provision organised on different days/times. Meanwhile, the majority of RCCs continue to provide support services exclusively for women and girls, while those few that have developed services for men nevertheless stress that their main work is in providing specialist support services 'for women, by women'. This would again suggest that RCCs in Britain have for the most part effectively managed to retain feminist needs-based services for female survivors of rape and sexual abuse. Feminist RCCs are very aware of their tenuous position regarding funding, choosing to identify themselves explicitly as 'woman-centred' feminist voluntary groups, while at the same time organising in a variety of ways to protect essential services and ensure the continuation and expansion of funding sources.

Victim Support Schemes, unlike RCCs and other alternative support services, operate in partnership with the police and receive generous funding from the Home Office (Rock, 1990). VSS have moved into the area of rape and sexual assault, the implications of which are discussed in further detail below. Central government has supported – and indeed encouraged – the rapid growth of VSS during the 1980s, reflecting increasing concern for crime victims on the part of criminal justice agencies and in the wider society (Shapland *et al.*, 1985; Maguire and Pointing, 1988; Mawby and Gill, 1987; Walklate, 1989; Gill and Mawby, 1990; Rock, 1990). My national survey found that RCCs, in contrast to VSS, are typically funded through a combination of short-term grants, joint financing by social services and health authorities, grants from the local police authority and other funders with an interest in service provision for rape victims. These funding sources are notoriously insecure and make it very difficult for workers to plan strategies and support services in the long term. Most RCCs in England and Wales survive on a mixture of such grants, together with local fundraising, trust monies and charitable donations. In terms of government funding, RCCs can be said to have been marginalised in favour of VSS, which work in close partnership with the police; indeed, VSS are dependent on their relationship with the police for NAVSS affiliation and continued Home Office funding.

Relations with the police

The police have initiated a number of reforms and practical measures in terms of their treatment of rape 'victims', including victim examination suites, specialist services for victims of rape and domestic violence, training of women officers, and the recruitment of more women police surgeons. In this sense, the police can be seen to have responded to the demands of feminists and the wider public for improved treatment of women who have suffered violence, particularly at the point of contact when women report rape, sexual assault or domestic violence (Rock, 1988; Adler, 1991; Dobash and Dobash, 1992). Nevertheless, these 'new initiatives' have been criticised by feminist writers for not going far enough (Radford, 1989; Hanmer, Radford and Stanko, 1989; Dunhill, 1989). Such changes in police policy and practices, together with ad hoc reforms in the treatment of rape victims in the wider criminal justice system (including the legal recognition of rape within marriage), have emerged as a result of successful public campaigns by feminist action groups and grassroots organisations. However, despite changes in police policy in the treatment of women who have experienced men's violence, nevertheless the majority of RCCs reported difficulties in their working relationships with local police.

As noted above, RCCs have been characterised in the main as both anti-men and anti-police (Blair, 1985), with a few centres singled out as 'acceptable' agencies for police referral (in that they are characterised as 'less extreme' or 'non-feminist' organisations). However, my research has shown that many RCCs struggle to negotiate working relationships with local police in the context of police antipathy towards them. In the course of interviews with police officers, RCCs have often been described to me as 'extreme' feminist groups that typically persuade women not to report rape and sexual offences. Conversely, in interviews with RCC workers, a few have reported police pressure to breach the fundamental principle of confidentiality regarding women who use their services. Thus rather than keeping RCCs 'at arm's length' (Rock, 1990: 182), there is evidence that in some cases investigating officers have sought information or 'intelligence' in order to build up a profile of known local rapists, primarily to facilitate the investigation of reported rape cases. Furthermore, there is a prevalent view within police forces in Britain that RCCs are deliberately holding back information that could be used to assist investigation. These pressures have been fiercely resisted by RCCs in the face of the increased likelihood of reduction, or possible loss, of funding and aggravating difficulties in working relations. The issue of confidentiality is central to RCC service provision. Indeed, the majority of RCCs require volunteers to sign a statement requiring workers not to disclose any details or information about clients to outside agencies. It is also felt strongly, in line with the feminist counselling model of empowerment, that it is for women who have been raped to choose whether or not to disclose information to the police or other statutory agencies. At the same time, rape survivors should not in any way be held accountable for the actions of men who choose to rape. This highlights the different roles and service philosophies of the police and RCCs. The former are necessarily engaged in the detection and criminal investigation of reported sexual offences, while the latter primarily offer confidential counselling and support services for all women who have been raped or sexually assaulted – whether they choose to report to the police or not – and no matter how long ago the offences took place. Indeed, RCCs are frequently exhorted by local police to persuade or cajole women to report rape or sexual assault; although this is perhaps understandable given the police role, it nevertheless ignores the importance that RCC workers place on their commitment to non-directive support and the empowerment of rape survivors. All RCCs support women who wish to report rape and sexual assault to the police, but they would never put pressure on women to do so. Another area of concern expressed by RCC workers and women police officers alike is that of the role of women officers in service provision for rape survivors. The increasing involvement of women police officers in the long-term care and support of rape survivors needs to be welcomed cautiously given their statutory role of criminal investigation and hence the possibility of confusion for victims. It may well be more appropriate for women to be referred to RCCs for long-term support. This need not preclude women who have been raped from choosing to maintain close links with supportive women officers. Nevertheless, officers have a responsibility to advise women that they have a statutory role and they may not always be able to maintain such support if, for example, they are stationed elsewhere or moved to another case.

VSS and support for rape victims

It has been argued that the diversity and fragmentation of alternative voluntary organisations including RCCs has led to opportunism by organisations such as VSS who are better resourced and work in close partnership with local government (Mawby and Gill, 1987; Rock, 1990).

VSS are traditional voluntary organisations that sprang out of the crime victim movement in Britain (Maguire and Pointing, 1988; Mawby and Gill, 1987; Rock, 1990). They were established primarily to offer practical and emotional support to victims of crime and their families. They offer advice and help around issues such as compensation, police and court procedures and reparation schemes including victim–offender mediation. As stated earlier, VSS work in close partnership with the police, relying in the main on police referrals. One characteristic that VSS share in common with RCCs is that they are not homogeneous organisations; they vary in terms of service philosophy, provision and resources. Nevertheless, all those schemes affiliated to the National Association of Victim Support Schemes (NAVSS) offer primarily short-term counselling to crime victims based on a crisis intervention model. There would appear then to be a disjunction between, on the one hand, VSS espousal of the short-term crisis intervention model for the support of crime victims (see below for further discussion) and, on the other, their increasing involvement with victims of rape and sexual assault who often experience long-term effects and reactions associated specifically with sexual violence (London Rape Crisis Centre, 1984; Kelly, 1988).

In 1982 NAVSS had responded to pressure by central government to extend service provision to victims of rape and serious violence (Rock, 1990) although some VSS in London had been accepting police referrals of rape cases since the beginning of the 1980s (Corbett and Hobdell, 1988). When NAVSS submitted proposals for Home Office funding in 1983 they claimed that 'in the absence of any other credible body concerned with the victims of crime . . . we are beginning to identify areas of special need such as victims of rape. . .' (Rock, 1990: 184). The NAVSS Conference in 1985 passed a resolution that VSS should provide support for female victims of sexual assault with reference to Dr Claire Corbett's report on the effectiveness of VSS in helping victims of rape (Corbett and Hobdell, 1988).

By 1986 NAVSS had convened a Working Party to consider provision of support for victims of rape and sexual assault. Subsequently, VSS have increasingly taken on this area of support encouraged by the police and Home Office (Mawby and Gill, 1987; Rock, 1990). The NAVSS *Training Manual for Supporting Female Victims of Sexual Assault* exhorts volunteers to advise victims of rape and sexual assault to report the offence to the police in order to assist the detection and arrest of offenders (NAVSS, 1986). While acknowledging the service provision offered by RCCs, nevertheless it is argued that '. . . although hitherto Victim Support has avoided duplicating existing services to victims, in this particular category of victimisation offering women a choice is of greater importance' (NAVSS, 1986: 3). The manual refers to a Consultation Paper entitled 'Confidentiality', which is forwarded to all VSS and where it is claimed that '. . . freedom to confide is safeguarded, in general terms, by agency policy, grounded in the code of practice. . .' (1986: 11). Nevertheless, the manual goes on to state that:

Victims of sexual assault have an extremely strong need to trust that their often painful confidence will not be openly discussed. However this particular type of personal crime may produce many strains on the principle of confidentiality. This can be specially highlighted where a victim has decided not to report the offence to the police and may well know the identity of her attacker. Thus schemes approaching this area of work should study this Paper carefully paying particular attention to the section 'Dealing with Difficulties: when confidentiality may have to be breached'. . . . It has been the experience of Working Party members that precedents do not exist in this area and that should such difficult choices arise, schemes will perhaps need to balance very carefully the needs of the victims against the protection of society (NAVSS, 1986: 11).

However, on the following page of the manaual an example is given of an information leaflet for women, including a section headed 'How can victim support help you?'. Here we are told that:

Any woman can become the victim of sexual assault, and the feelings which result can be complex, confusing and deeply disturbing. Many women appreciate talking in confidence with a sensitive outsider who will listen sympathetically to their feelings and concerns. We understand that not all women will have reported the incident to the police and in no way would we *pressure* anyone to do so (underlined in manual, NAVSS, 1986: 12).

This acknowledgement of the possibility for breach of confidentiality on the part of volunteers is particularly worrying in the light of the increasing involvement of VSS in this area of work. Furthermore, it is a matter of great concern that volunteers, albeit vetted by the police, should have access to police information about the nature of sexual offences together with personal details about the victim who may or may not have knowingly consented to contact from VSS.

Clearly, victims of sexual offences should have a choice of agencies to turn to if they need advice and support. Nevertheless, the expansion of VSS into areas of rape and domestic violence suggests a move towards the monopolisation of service provision, given the statutory support and very generous Home Office funding of VSS to the exclusion of other agencies offering victim support (Rock, 1990).

While for RCCs the bulk of referrals are self-referrals, VSS rely in the main on police referrals, either through an automatic referral system of all crimes recorded (including in some police forces rape, sexual assault and domestic violence) or through selective procedures on the part of VSS coordinators which, in turn, are often dependent on the availability of volunteers. Nevertheless, VSS are developing drop-in centres nationally and are seeking to increase the rate of self-referrals.

In comparison to RCCs in Britain, VSS have only recently moved into the area of service provision for rape victims. In the course of interviews with VSS counsellors, concerns have been expressed that they are inadequately trained to provide such specialist, long-term support for this client group. Indeed, it could be seen as somewhat ironic that some VSS are finding it necessary to approach local RCCs to provide the relevant training or, alternatively, are seeking advice from statutory agencies including the police who, in turn, have frequently received their training from RCCs.

VSS training in the area of rape is centred on Rape Trauma Syndrome (RTS) (Burgess and Holstrom, 1979), a crisis intervention model of counselling support for rape victims. This model is very different from the often long-term, non-directive support offered by RCCs. The RTS model was imported from the USA and is based on an identified Victim Trauma Syndrome, where victims are considered to go through a number of stages in the aftermath of an assault or burglary or other crimes against the person. It is believed that with supportive counselling victims can be helped to resume 'normality' and come to terms with their traumatic experience (for further discussion, see Chapter 2 in this volume). Indeed, many RCCs find aspects of RTS useful as a counselling model as it describes a range of responses that rape survivors may experience in both the short and long term following the trauma of sexual violence. However, the implication of this model for the counselling and support of rape survivors is that women who are not seen as coping, who are not 'back to normal' after a few months, are referred on to other agencies including psychiatric services (NAVSS, 1986). This has been criticised as indicative of the growing tendency on the part of mainstream service providers to medicalise and pathologise rape and to ignore the complexity of responses of rape survivors and their struggles to cope with the aftermath of sexual violence (Kelly, 1988, 1989a; see also Chapter 2 in this volume). RCCs are critical of the implication in the RTS model that '. . . with reassurance and practical help, women are usually able to regain control over their lives within a few months . . . [while] . . . for some, the process of recovery is not too disrupting . . . making the journey from victim to "survivor" in a remarkably short period and against many obstacles' (Corbett and Hobdell, 1988: 55).

VSS volunteers are trained in mixed male and female groups and it is considered appropriate in some circumstances for male volunteers to visit and counsel female victims of rape and sexual assault, albeit where female volunteers may not be available. Furthermore, VSS literature in this field has adopted the language used by RCCs, referring in some instances, as in the extract above, to 'survivors' while at times acknowledging the long-term effects of rape and sexual assault. However, the model used remains primarily one of short-term crisis intervention, while the central focus is on supporting the crime victim.

I would concur with Mawby and Gill that while VSS may well seek to widen their role by supporting victims in cases that go to court, nevertheless '. . . where long term services are required coordinators should . . . feel able to refer victims to other specialist agencies where appropriate', including RCCs (1987: 232).

There is evidence from my research that such referrals are occurring in many areas. Indeed, the apparent caution expressed by some VSS cordinators about developing services into areas such as rape, sexual assault and domestic violence may well be a reflection of tensions between different levels of VSS organisation. Clearly, at national level the NAVSS is keen to expand support services for all victims of crime, encouraged by government policy, and to this end pressure has been applied to county-wide VSS federations to monitor and control the quality of service provision, including the coordination and centralisation of training of local groups. At the same time, local VSS coordinators have expressed fears of loss of autonomy and there is evidence from the research of some resistance to directives imposed from above, particularly at county level. However this tension is ultimately played out within VSS, I would argue with Mawby and Gill that alternative support services including Women's Aid refuges and RCCs should not be 'freezed out' (sic) (1987: 231).

RCC responses and strategies for survival

RCCs have over time necessarily developed strategies to survive the difficulties encountered in the interface with statutory and voluntary agencies. They have had to learn how to play the 'funding game' and how to work with the agenda of local statutory and government agencies. In some cases, as indicated earlier, this has led to fundamental changes in the organisational set-up, moving away from non-hierarchical, collective modes of working towards more of a structured, line-management approach with a clearly defined division of labour, particularly where RCCs may have several

full-time paid workers. Brenton has highlighted the problems
of internal democracy for voluntary groups, where decision-
making tends to devolve out of necessity to full-time paid
workers involved in the day-to-day running of the organisation (Brenton, 1985).

In addition to pressures facing RCCs from outside the
feminist movement, there have been difficulties and issues
faced by centres and other autonomous women's groups that
have been acknowledged within the feminist movement.
Differences between women have led to fears of fragmentation of the women's movement and at times to bewilderment
on the part of women committed to providing feminist
support services in the face of the wider ideological and
political 'cold climate' and generalised backlash against
feminism (see the Introduction in this volume). While
acknowledging the tensions and contradictions that have
fragmented the feminist movement along lines of race, class,
sexuality and other identified differences between women
(Ramazanoglu, 1989; Kelly, 1989a), recent research, including
my study, indicates that autonomous women's groups are
emerging as stronger and more coordinated support services
that, on the whole, manage to retain a distinctive feminist
service philosophy based on a woman-centred, anti-racist
approach (Kelly, 1988).

The survival of RCCs in Britain may well depend on the
current development of regional, and ultimately national,
federation along the lines of Women's Aid refuges for battered
women (see Chapter 3 in this volume). The issue of federation
surfaced regularly on agenda at RCC conferences throughout
the 1980s. It appears to be emerging in the 1990s as a viable
strategy for resisting managerialist pressures and further
marginalisation. At the same time, some RCCs (notably
those who do not identify themselves as explicitly feminist
centres) see federation as a threat to their autonomy, evident
in concerns expressed by some RCC workers about the
implications of affiliation to a national umbrella organisation.

Other centres, managed or overseen by committees representing statutory bodies, may feel that federation is at odds with
'effective' multi-agency working.

In addition, RCCs are forming alliances and inter-agency
networks with national women's groups, including the
National Association of Women's Organisations, and with
charitable organisations. These agencies may act in an
advisory capacity, supporting RCCs in their bids for
charitable status, in the development towards federation,
and in applying pressure for central government funding.

In some cases, as stated earlier, employers or their
representatives on executive management committees have
required organisational changes of centres (Mawby and Gill,
1987). While these formal structures have imposed requirements on RCCs for greater accountability (for example,
showing demand for services, producing reports, statistics and
audited accounts), they have also in many cases facilitated the
development of specialist support services. Such initiatives
include employing project workers in areas such as HIV/AIDS
work, service provision for black, Asian and minority ethnic
women, working with prostitute women who are at risk of
violence from punters and pimps alike (see Chapter 6 in this
volume), community outreach and education work, developing training packages and interpretor services and, in a few
RCCs, employing female or male counsellors to provide
services specifically for men who have been sexually assaulted.

Nevertheless, this is not to minimise the problems for
feminist voluntary groups who may be diverted from meeting
the needs of women service users by the demands of statutory
funding requirements (Mawby and Gill, 1987: 70) and who
may be required to '. . . "choose" to modify their ideological
stance' (1987: 73). It may well be the case that British RCCs
will emerge as 'relatively autonomous' women's groups
(Brenton, 1985), retaining a degree of independence from
local government bodies and statutory agencies while
continuing to develop feminist services specifically for female
survivors of sexual violence.

Conclusion

Earlier in this chapter I posed questions concerning the future for RCCs in Britain as acknowledged specialist service providers in the face of economic, political, organisational and ideological pressures towards loss of autonomy, marginalisation or incorporation into local statutory agencies. Further, competition for funding sources from organisations seeking to duplicate services has added to the difficulties experienced by many RCCs amid increasing fears of marginalisation.

I have suggested that RCCs, while not homogeneous organisations, have had some success in resisting or negotiating such pressures, while for the most part retaining a distinctively feminist, woman-centred service provision. Many RCCs are devising practical strategies in the short term to raise their public profile, while at the same time organising and applying pressure in the long term to secure funding mechanisms in order to enhance the quality of service provision for female survivors of rape and sexual assault.

It is to be hoped that statutory agencies such as the police, health and social services, together with traditional voluntary agencies such as VSS that work in close partnership with statutory organisations, will offer greater support to autonomous women's groups than has been evident in the past. It is not enough simply to pay lip service to the expertise of autonomous women's groups while espousing the rhetoric of 'respect for different service philosophies' and/or the 'importance of offering choice to the consumer/client'. Agencies acknowledging the work of RCCs should make it policy to refer women to centres where appropriate and when women have expressed a need for counselling and support. The initial findings from my national research indicate that 'multi-agency cooperation' may indeed be more rhetoric than reality in terms of the coordination of support services for rape survivors. RCCs will need to be ever vigilant to ensure that funding and other statutory support is not eroded and that a distinctively feminist service philosophy is not diluted. This inevitably presents difficulties for RCCs, which need to consider carefully the terms under which they enter multi-agency working and 'partnerships' with local statutory and government agencies. RCCs in Britain have so far, for the most part and not without considerable struggle, survived the organisational, ideological and structural pressures outlined in this chapter. Consequently, I would argue that they can emerge as stronger and more strategic organisations, in the sense of continuing to build upon established supportive networks and alliances within and outside the feminist movement, while mindful of the difficulties encountered by feminist groups that have entered the arena of multi-agency working. Thus it is to be hoped that RCCs will secure a better resourced future built on a proven track record as the frontline providers of distinctively feminist support services for female survivors of sexual violence.

Notes

1. The research focuses on the interface between Rape Crisis Centres (RCCs), the police and Victim Support Schemes (VSS) in England and Wales, using a combination of national surveys and an in-depth case study based on interviews with RCC workers, police officers, VSS coordinators and volunteers in one police authority. It is proposed to conduct a comparative study focusing on a different police authority, mindful of proposed changes in the structure and organisation of police forces in England and Wales.
2. Statutory and traditional voluntary agencies working within or closely with the criminal justice system tend to refer to the 'crime victim', or more specifically here the 'rape victim', whereas RCCs and women who have experienced sexual violence often prefer to use the term 'survivor' when referring to women and children who have experienced sexual abuse. Feminists have

argued that the term 'survivor' is more empowering than that of 'victim', expressing instead the capacity of women to resist and struggle against male sexual violence (Kelly, 1988; Stanko, 1985; Kelly and Radford, 1987). While recognising the significance of using the term 'survivor', RCCs nevertheless acknowledge that some women who have been raped or sexually abused prefer to use the term 'victim' in the sense of perceiving themselves as victims of a criminal offence, regardless of whether the crime was reported to the police. This is clearly not to imply in any way passivity or blame on the part of the woman, nor to detract from the criminal responsibility of men who choose to perpetrate violence against women and children.

3. The postal survey of fifty-nine RCCs in England and Wales was conducted in 1989 and received responses from thirty-eight centres. The survey examined service provisions, funding, the interface with statutory and voluntary organisations, organisational modes and strategies of resistance in the context of changing economic, political and ideological pressures facing autonomous women's groups.

4. The responses from RCCs in the survey show that RCCs are primarily feminist service providers offering support and counselling to female survivors of men's sexual violence. Some centres claim in publicity literature an explicit commitment to the long-term goal of ending men's violence to women and children. In many cases, however, RCCs do not have the resources to engage in sustained campaigning work, although for the most part they are supportive of organisations such as WAR (Women Against Rape) and WAVAW (Women Against Violence Against Women) who are explicitly politically motivated and actively committed to ending male violence.

5. For example, one of the RCCs in the case study has produced an annual report (1992) which highlights 'The reputation of the . . . Centre as a caring, skilled and professional service. . .'. Included are statistics compiled on service use over the previous year, showing an overall increase in demand of 16 per cent. The report goes on to state that 'With the impending implementation of the Community Care Act in April 1993, the . . . Centre has found it necessary to adopt a clearly defined client catchment area because of the anticipated increase in client referrals.' This centre adopts a line management structure, headed by a director

with the assistance of two specialist paid workers. The centre is overseen by an Executive Management Committee made up of representatives from local statutory bodies including the police, health and social services.

2

Professionalising the Response to Rape

Marian Foley

Introduction

Over the last decade we have witnessed some very public changes in police policy around rape, child abuse and, more recently, 'wife abuse'. There has also been a massive growth in professional service provision for women who have experienced male sexual violence. This growth was in response to feminist criticisms of the inadequate and negative treatment women received from the criminal justice system and the medical and mental health services they turned to for help. Feminists were particularly critical of police attitudes towards women reporting rape and campaigned vigorously for changes in police practice. Many of the practical changes called for have been implemented by police forces and have come to represent a new and more sensitive police approach to rape investigations. However, in this chapter I will examine the changing features of professional service provision and argue that it represents only a limited response to feminist concerns. The practical improvements feminists campaigned for have largely been met, but the political analysis of male sexual violence underpinning the service response has not changed. Rape has been redefined as a medical issue requiring professional expertise. The result has been a growth in service provision that has sought to pathologise and individualise women's reactions to rape.

Feminism and professionalisation

Feminism put male sexual violence against women firmly on the political agenda by developing, and continuing to develop, a political analysis of male sexual violence that is based on women's experiences. As women began to speak out about male violence, they also began to talk about the inadequate and often punitive response they received from the agencies and individual professional workers they turned to for help. Women were frequently blamed for provoking male violence and men's violence was typically excused and/or normalised. Feminists challenged both this orthodox understanding of male violence and the way it shaped service provision. They developed a system of support networks and services such as Women's Aid refuges, Rape Crisis Centres (RCCs) and safe houses for survivors of child sexual abuse (see Chapters 1 and 3 in this volume). These services quickly multiplied into a large-scale movement for social change, which campaigned vigorously for male violence against women to be taken seriously, for changes in the criminal justice system and for appropriate service provision based on women's needs. They added a collective strength to individual women's experiences that was hard to ignore.

The police and other professionals have increasingly begun to respond to feminist criticisms and have rapidly expanded their service provision to incorporate many feminist issues. However, they have not adopted a feminist political analysis of male violence. Instead, they have used their professional status as a means of marginalising feminist services and silencing feminist analysis and debate. In taking on the issues, they are attempting to take control over these particular areas of work and change the definition of the 'problem' to be managed and the parameters of the debate.

Professionalism can be defined in terms of the following attributes: specialist knowledge based on years of formal education; unique skills and training; service altruism and neutrality of expertise (McKinlay, 1973; Esland, 1980). These characteristics, though, are not restricted to professional services and can exist independently of professional status (Freidson,1970). Professionalism may be viewed as a process whereby professionals seek to gain a monopoly over certain areas of work. The trappings of professionalism are used by particular occupations to advance their interests and their control over the performance of certain tasks. The specialised knowledge and skills they claim create the basis for prestige and social distinction between the 'expert' and the 'client' (Turner, 1987). This specialised knowledge creates a mystique of exclusivity around their work: only they can do the job and it is dangerous for anyone else to try (Goode, 1969). Occupations like social work and nursing that are semi-professional or paraprofessional will attempt to pursue full professional status and the benefits that go with it, even though they remain subordinate to the professions on which they model themselves (Freidson, 1970).

In terms of service provision for women who have experienced sexual violence, professional groups have sought to reassert their control over this area of work. In doing so they have taken on feminist areas of work, but explicitly rejected the political understandings underpinning it. This attempt to take over the debate is based partly on the challenge feminism has made to their professional practice. Feminism has confronted their knowledge, methods, the value-laden nature of their assumptions and ultimately the effectiveness of their service provision. In response, professional groups have used professionalisation and medicalisation as strategies to gain control of the problem from feminists and to redefine it in terms of women's illness rather than men's sexual violence.

The professionalisation and medicalisation of rape

The attempts by professionals to take over service provision for women who have been raped has a political motive that is often hidden beneath the concern expressed for 'victims'. By focusing exclusively on 'treating' women who have been raped, professionals have shifted the definition of the problem away from male violence, and the process by which it is legitimated and normalised, on to women's responses to that violence. The legitimate forum for treatment becomes medicine. There has been an increasing trend towards redefining all aspects of male sexual violence as medical problems. For example, women's reactions to male violence have been pathologised by medical labels like the 'battered women's syndrome' and the Rape Trauma Syndrome (RTS). These labels have turned women's reactions to male violence into medical diseases (Edwards, 1989). In line with this shift and the emphasis on women's 'illness' comes the corresponding emphasis on medical expertise and the need for trained medical intervention to effect a 'cure'. Women are now expected to put their faith in the hands of medical professionals and a hospital location has become an appropriate site for 'treatment' programmes or counselling services. In relation to adult survivors of child sexual abuse, Armstrong (1990) has argued that the fact of survivors speaking out has not, as they hoped, challenged male power, but has instead opened up new ground for therapeutic intervention. The result has been a rapid move away from defining child abuse as a criminal act in favour of labelling child abuse as a sickness:

> We called it traditional, they called it deviant. We called it criminal, they called it sick. And the offenders – . . . when they finally caught their breath – they called it a big lie. Our political understanding was all but obliterated (Armstrong, 1990: 50).

The same refusal to look at male sexual violence and the power systems and ideologies that encourage and condone it can also be applied to rape and wife assault.

This shift in emphasis and the consequent depoliticisation of sexual violence have largely been achieved by making 'victims' the focus of treatment. Women's reactions have been pathologised. The shift has been subtle because on the surface such service provision appears to offer a similar, but 'professional', service to feminist RCCs as both seek to provide counselling services for women who have been raped. However, the type of service provided by medical professionals is very different because their focus and their definition of the problem are significantly different from those of many feminist RCCs. Professionals have almost exclusively started from the premise that it is women's reaction to male violence that is the problem to be addressed and managed. Medical expertise becomes essential to a woman's recovery and her return to 'normality'. This particular understanding is hard to challenge because superficially it appears to be supporting the 'victim'.

This interest in and focus on women's reactions to rape stems from the work of Burgess and Holstrom (1974), whose influential study of women admitted to the emergency ward of a Boston hospital after being raped identified a number of common reactions to rape; these were condensed under the label of Rape Trauma Syndrome (RTS). As Kelly points out: 'No-one has questioned conceptualising the impact of rape as anything other than a medical model' (Kelly, 1989a: 11).

Rape has been described as a 'classic crisis situation' (Hoff and Williams, 1975), and the crisis intervention model for counselling women who have been raped, as outlined by Burgess and Holstrom (1974), has received a great deal of support (Roehl and Gray, 1984; Ben-Zavi and Horsfall, 1985). A healthy woman's response to rape has been plotted and treatment targets set accordingly (Katz, 1979). Much of the research into the long-term effects of rape has identified its effects as: 'Discrete physiological and/or psychological changes which could be measured by "objective" psychological tests' (Kelly, 1988: 159).

The conceptualisation of effects in this way fails to account for the complexity of women's experiences. Women's reactions to rape are effectively reduced to a series of mathematical equations that provide the basis for treatment. For example, women not only suffer from RTS, they also suffer from 'post-traumatic stress disorders'. The complexity of women's experiences of male violence has thus been reduced to a set of individual symptoms that, once understood, can be cured by the medical profession.

Recovery is defined by the medical experts as helping women to return to the pre-rape state. The goal of medical treatment becomes one of getting women back to 'normal', which inevitably means getting women to act as if the rape has not happened. This medical goal is inappropriate because it fails to acknowledge that women's responses to male sexual violence may lead to 'permanent changes in attitudes, behaviour and circumstances' (Kelly, 1988). Instead, it chooses to view these responses as negative, irrational and in need of change, especially if they include an opting out of heterosexuality, temporarily or permanently, and a mistrust of men. A healthy response to rape and a successful resolution of the crisis is clearly linked to a return to functioning heterosexuality. Women who choose celibacy on a temporary or permanent basis and women who make a positive decision to become lesbians, are viewed negatively. However, for the women concerned, they represent positive choices which are part of the recovery process (Heller, 1990).

If the rape happened some time ago, the after-effects of rape are conceptualised as 'conditioned fear reactions' which lead to changes in central beliefs 'about safety, esteem, trust, intimacy and control' (Koss and Harvey, 1991: 177). These fear reactions can be modified by 'stress inoculation therapy': the aim being to get women to behave as if the rape has never happened (Kelly, 1989a). Women are encouraged to trust men because women's distrust of men is viewed as unreasonable and problematic. Women's response to male violence may be diagnosed as psychotic and the behaviour modification to rectify it may include the use of psychosurgery (Hudson, 1987). This demonstrates the gulf between medical under-standings of rape and women's understandings of the world they live in. For women living in a society where male violence against women is endemic, mistrust of men may not only be realistic but healthy:

> I say that for women living in our society as it exists, the successful resolution is basic mistrust, at least if you don't want to be a rape victim. This perspective makes life difficult and unpleasant, but it is what we mean when we say women are oppressed (Bart, 1989: 66).

For women living under this oppression, negotiating personal safety is an everyday reality (Stanko, 1990). But medical science avoids acknowledging the extent of male violence and its normalisation and concentrates on teaching women how to live in the world as it is presently structured. Women are expected to come to terms with the world rather than to challenge it. In depoliticising rape, men and male power are protected. The medicalisation of rape ensures that rape is perceived as a problem affecting individual women (Toronto Rape Crisis, 1985). This is not to suggest that there is no place for individual counselling, but to argue that individual solutions are not the answer to the systematic abuse of women and children and do not encourage change: 'When you are looking at systematic, system-endorsed power abuse, individualized solutions – exclusively individualized solutions – are antithetical to change' (Armstrong, 1990: 53).

The crux of the issue is that what represents a successful medical resolution to the problem may not translate into a successful resolution of the problem for the women concerned. The growth of medical interest in providing a service for women who have experienced rape has resulted in a number of countries setting up Sexual Assault Referral Centres (SARCs). SARCs have been established in Australia, Canada and the USA for a number of years. These Centres were set up in response to feminist campaigns for better facilities for women and girls who had experienced rape. In New South Wales, Australia, SARCs have been in operation since 1978. They are usually situated in hospitals in urban areas and community health centres in rural areas. SARCs aim to provide crisis counselling; immediate medical treatment if necessary; facilitate and enhance the collection of forensic evidence and provide ongoing counselling (Earle, 1988). These SARCs are often feminist, but differ in approach, service provision and delivery and politics.

The impact of professionalisation

The professionalisation of services has sought to depoliticise rape, not only by providing alternative services but by incorporating existing feminist services. When large-scale funding became available in North America and Canada, it radically changed the nature of existing feminist service provision and 'in too many cases the revolution was over' (Pride, 1991: 114). The work of feminist groups became tied to the power of the purse string, which often stipulated changes in organisational structure, employees and language. The change of language often denoted a shift in the definition of the problem, a toning down of political commitment and a very different ethos behind service delivery. In addition, there has been an increased dominance of the therapeutic model which blames male violence on personality deficiencies in women's characters. Failure to comply with the more traditional ways of working have resulted in feminist groups being taken over by professional workers (Pride, 1981). The result has been the growing conformity of previously radical groups and the adoption of a social services approach to their work, which turns women into social problems and ignores the real issue of men's violence (see Chapter 3 in this volume).

Largely in response to feminist demands during the late 1970s, the Canadian government began to fund RCCs. As rape became an important source of funding, social service agencies became interested. The availability of large-scale funding has divided the feminist movement into two camps: those that have adopted a social service approach and employed professional administrators, psychologists and therapists; and those groups that have resisted such attempts to professionalise and that have kept their original vision of providing a support service alongside attempts to challenge social institutions that encourage and condone male sexual violence. Whatever individual RCCs decide, they will be forced to chose between a more specialised professional model or retain feminist goals with the risk of losing their funding (Toronto Rape Crisis, 1985). There is ample evidence from North America and Canada to suggest that if radical groups resist being professionalised and thus incorporated into existing state structures, they are in much greater danger of being marginalised (Price, 1988; Toronto Rape Crisis, 1985; Schechter, 1981).

RCCs in England have not as yet come under the same pressure to conform as they have never attracted large-scale government funding. However, this does not mean that feminist RCCs have not experienced any competition, rather that the bulk of this competition has come from other voluntary organisations, namely the Victim Support Schemes (VSS) (see Chapter 1 in this volume). When VSSs were initially set up, the focus of their work was largely limited to dealing with burglary and bogus callers, but their scope widened during the latter half of the 1980s to include rape and sexual assault (Corbett and Hobdell, 1988). The number of police referrals to VSS and the importance attached to the work of VSS will vary both between and within police forces, but, as police-backed voluntary groups, VSS are often considered to be a better alternative to RCCs. The first police-supported SARC in Britain was unveiled in December 1986 and has since become an exemplar of good police practice (*Guardian*, 5 December 1990). Some RCCs have responded to this competition by adopting a more professional approach.

SARCs in Britain

SARCs are a very recent development in Britain, with only one currently existing; this is situated in a large maternity hospital in the north of England. This SARC was based on the Australian model in terms of location and operation. However, it differs from its Australian counterparts in one very important respect: the level of police involvement. The British SARC is a joint police and medical initiative and police referrals make up the bulk of the Centre's work. In New South Wales the police were not involved in setting up the SARC, although interdepartmental guidelines require police officers to refer women to them. Despite these guidelines, the Australian police have been unwilling to refer women to SARC and, when they do, they refer only those women they believe have been raped (Bureau of Crime Statistics and Research, 1985).

The British SARC is a good empirical example of the two central tendencies – the professionalisation and medicalisation of rape – outlined above. It was presented through public meetings, media coverage and publicity material as a Centre offering professional medical help to women who have been 'seriously' sexually assaulted (SARC leaflet, n.d.). The counsellors employed were described as: 'Women who have a wide experience in counselling the victims of sexual abuse. They are professionals in their field of work.' (SARC leaflet, n.d).[1]

Establishing the SARC fulfilled a number of objectives for those involved, although the impetus came from two interested parties: the police and various medical professionals. The primary motivation was to provide suitable accommodation where women could be medically examined outside a police environment. The Chief Constable hoped it would 'dispel unwarranted scepticism of police procedure' (Report of the Chief Constable, 18 April 1986), and that the facilities offered would encourage more women to report to the police (White, 1986b; *Brief*, 1986: 1). The SARC would also provide better forensic facilities and enhance the collection of medical evidence. Improved treatment of the women would produce better witness accounts. According to its director, the forensic service is the 'cornerstone' of the Centre (SARC Open Forum, 1989). The local police perceived that setting up the SARC would not only dispel criticism, but produce much wider benefits: 'A spin-off is of course that the force has greater credibility in this area than it previously enjoyed' (document to the Home Office, 1987).

The location of the SARC in a hospital was extremely important because it displaced the issue of police practice into a medical debate (Foley, 1991: 204). It was also perceived to be a means of controlling the spread of hepatitis B and HIV/AIDS. The police believed that the testing of sexually transmitted diseases by the SARC would help in their containment. At the same time they felt a hospital-based location had the facility for admissions and could deal with medical emergencies. As a police facility, part of the SARC's role was to pass information on crimes committed to the police (SARC Open Forum, 1986). Besides these practical advantages, the SARC also fed into certain taken-for-granted assumptions about the appropriate nature of a service for women who have experienced rape. One such assumption was that a professional service should employ nurses. This was partly because it was felt that nurses would have experience in dealing with 'ladies' problems' and partly because they believed that women who have been raped are 'psychiatrically ill' (Foley, 1991: 202).

Despite some superficial similarities to the RCCs (it is headed by a woman and only employs women counsellors), the SARC has striven to separate itself from feminist explanations of male sexual violence. The SARC's understanding of rape is located firmly within Rape Trauma Syndrome (RTS), treatment of which is viewed as the solution to the problem. It uses gender-neutral language when discussing its work and stresses that the Centre is open to men as well as women. Explanations given for this are that the feminist bias of RCCs puts women off men and that the Centres are anti-police (Duddle, 1985). The director of the SARC recognises that feminist organisations have had a role to play, but would 'seriously question whether they were/are the best means of providing such care' (Roberts, 1984).

In particular, RCCs are perceived as lacking the necessary professional skills. Nursing qualifications and experience in psycho-sexual counselling are deemed to be the appropriate qualifications for counsellors: 'It is envisaged that they will have nursing backgrounds and will have attended the (relevant) sexual counselling course' (Police/Community Liaison Unit, 8 September 1986) Indeed, the local psycho-sexual counselling course acted as an informal recruitment ground for SARC counsellors. All saw the acquisition of this qualification as an appropriate form of training for counselling women who have experienced rape. They were disappointed that they did not get to practise it as much as they had expected because the majority of women attending the Centre were young and without partners with whom to have a sexual problem (Foley, 1991: 251).

Counsellors also failed to question the appropriateness of psycho-sexual counselling or the assumptions behind it. For example, literature on psycho-sexual counselling contains implicit and explicit assumptions about what constitutes a 'real' sex act, which is rigidly reduced to penetration of the vagina by the penis. Sex therapy is geared towards teaching women how to enjoy penetration and views male sexual needs as paramount and 'natural'. Sexual problems are invariably reduced to women's inability to enjoy the act of penetration with a penis (McNeill, 1985). The aim of psycho-sexual literature and counselling is to teach women how to enjoy coitus (Jeffreys, 1990). Heterosexual relationships that do not involve penile penetration or where this is not the primary sex act are viewed as inferior. Lesbianism and homosexuality are treated as perverted and sexually immature (Storr, 1964; Kaplan, 1974; MacVaugh, 1979). There is no recognition that sexuality is socially constructed and fundamental to the 'construction of power relations between women and men' (Jackson, 1984: 45). The counsellors at the SARC perpetuate these assumptions in their work:

> Later we deal with problems such as vaginismus where the woman is unable to relax enough to have full sexual inter-course. Women also need to become orgasmic after rape, it is all part of getting their confidence back (*New Woman*, July 1989: 124).

In the same article it was made clear that having and maintaining heterosexual relationships was a sign of recovery.

How the SARC operates

It is these objectives and assumptions that have shaped the service delivery of the SARC. The Centre is a suite of rooms situated on the ground floor of a large maternity hospital, near the city centre. The suite of rooms includes an interview room, counselling room, medical examination room, shower and toilet. When the SARC opened, local police policy stated that if a woman comes into a police station to report a rape she should, after a brief initial questioning, be taken directly to the SARC. Here she should be medically examined and then allowed to shower and change her clothing before giving a full statement. In terms of facilities there is little difference between the SARC and the rape victim examination suites established by other police forces. The SARC is, however, different in two respects. First, it is open to anyone who wishes to use it, regardless of whether or not they report to the police. Second, the SARC employs counsellors. The bulk of the funding comes from the local police authority, while the health authority houses the Centre and pays for its day-to-day running costs.

The SARC offers telephone and face-to-face counselling, testing for sexually transmitted diseases, forensic medical examination, the morning-after pill and information on contraception. Counsellors will also accompany women to court. Calls out of office hours go through to the hospital radio room where a counsellor will be called out 'if necessary' (Foley, 1991:212). If it is a police referral, the police will call out a police surgeon and a counsellor. There are no facilities for women requesting a general medical check-up and doctors are not available for medical emergencies. Instead, women are advised to go to their GP or local casualty department (SARC letter, 1990).

Not surprisingly, given police objectives, the SARC is first and foremost for women reporting to the police: 'The first priority will be to provide superb facilities for those who do report rape to the police' (Community Health Council, 22 July 1986). Counsellors are encouraged to persuade women that this is the best course of action (ibid.) and success is clearly defined in these terms. Police referrals comprise the largest section of SARC referrals, representing 61 per cent of the total between 1986 and 1991 (SARC Progress Report, 1991). In turn, the police use the recorded increase in reported rapes to prove the success of the SARC (Chief Constable's Report, 1987). Despite such claims, it remains difficult to tell whether the number of rapes represents a real increase or simply a change in the way the police record such crimes (Scott and Dickens, 1989). It would also be wrong to conclude that improved facilities mean improved policing as rank and file officers resist and circumvent police policy (Stanko, 1989). Even officially approved behaviour can result in inappropriate and insensitive policing. Such was the case when one woman was arrested while at the SARC because she was wanted for questioning (SARC Management Committee Minutes, 14 November 1989). The Centre's service is limited to women who have been raped or seriously sexually assaulted; it thus excludes women who have been sexually abused as children. This was because these women were seen to need a different service and because they did not want the Centre to drown under a deluge of referrals (SARC Progress Report, 1988).

There are also women who may be excluded from using the SARC because of assumptions made about them. These include women who have a past psychiatric record and women whose rape is not believed. The argument is that these women need more specialised help (Foley, 1991: 223). The service offered also precludes women who cannot physically get to the SARC as the counsellors do not travel out.

Practice within the SARC also demonstrates a number of myths and assumptions about rape. Apparently rape is more distressing for professional women because they are used to having control over their lives (Foley, 1991: 233). Working-class women, by definition, get used to the 'knocks' of life and get over them faster than other women: 'It's the students who can't cope. It's the independent women used to control over their lives that it knocks the most. They take a hell of a long time to come to terms with it' (Foley, 1991: 234). It is also argued that the trauma of rape is worse for men than women as society expects men to fight back (SARC Open Forum, 1989). These assumptions are bound to have a bearing on practice: those who are in the most powerful positions – men by virtue of their maleness and middle-class women by virtue of their class, white people as a result of their race – are likely to be treated more sympathetically. Other groups of women – for example, working-class women or black women – are expected to experience less trauma.

Conclusion

The professionalisation and medicalisation of rape represent part of the wider backlash against feminism. Individual feminists and feminist organisations will need to develop more coherent and comprehensive strategies if we are successfully to challenge the reassertion of professional dominance. To achieve this we must develop better networking systems between feminist organisations. Most importantly, these organisations must find ways of supporting and validating individual feminists who work within the structures we want to change (Kelly, 1989a). In terms of developments like the British SARC, it seems unlikely that many police forces will have the money or the will to establish similar centres, at least at the moment. Indeed, the police have moved on to other areas of concern – for example, the establishment of Domestic Violence Units. We should also remember that SARCs in other countries have made attempts to move out of a medical setting and to make their services more accessible, so change is possible. In Britain, however, the police funding of the SARC is likely to prohibit any move in a similar direction. Ultimately, feminists must resist attempts to depoliticise rape and constantly challenge the development of service provision where the needs of women are held subservient to professional goals.

Note

1. The emphasis on professionalism and experience in counselling 'victims of sexual abuse' is very misleading and inaccurate. When the SARC initially opened, one of its counsellors was a psychologist and the other three were nurses who had no specific experience of counselling women who had been raped or sexually assaulted. Out of the four SARC counsellors I interviewed (the psychologist had left), only two had previous and limited contact with women who had been raped; none had any specific counselling skills in this area (Foley, 1991). They thus appear to have been deemed 'experienced' purely on the basis of their nursing qualifications.

3

The British Refuge Movement: The Survival of an Ideal?

Carol Lupton

Introduction

One of the major successes of the women's movement in Britain and the USA has been the redefinition of the phenomenon of wife assault from a private problem of individual familial relationships to a public issue with wider social and political determinants. In its location of men's violence against their wives[1] within the more general oppression of women by men, feminist analysis has successfully recast both the nature of the problem and, to an extent, the quality of society's response. In particular, in the absence of any effective statutory provision for the needs of women escaping violent partners, refuge movements both in the USA and the UK have developed extensive networks providing safe housing, support and advice for women and their children.[2]

Although sharing common origins and aims, the development of UK refuges and that of their American counterparts have been characterised by different historical tendencies. In the classification of organisational types, British refuges are typically identified as an enduring example of the radical 'social movement' model, at the other end of a continuum from more traditional 'social provision' agencies (Rose, 1985; Pahl, 1979; Mawby and Gill, 1987). In contrast, the experience of the battered women's shelters in the USA is often cited as an example of an initially feminist-inspired initiative that has evolved over time into a more conservative form of social problem management (Tierney, 1982; Ahrens, 1980; Ferraro, 1983; Morgan, 1985).

The 1980s and early 1990s, however, have presented those working in the UK refuge with new conflicts and challenges as a result of developments both within the movement and in its wider financial and political context. This chapter will outline these developments and examine their implications for the refuges and their work. In particular, it will examine the extent to which there are increasing pressures on British refuge groups to move closer to the American service provision model and will consider whether and in what ways such pressures have been resisted.

Models of provision

Mawby and Gill utilise four criteria in their classification of voluntary and independent agencies: relationship to statutory services; funding source; organisational goals and methods of providing help (1987: 72). At one end of a continuum of types are those whose relationship to the statutory services is oppositional rather than collaborative; who are largely self-supporting; whose goals and aims derive from their commitment to a wider 'social movement'; who eschew traditional models of helper and helped in favour of those that encourage empowerment and self-help and who seek to develop collectivist rather than hierarchical organisational forms (see Chapter 1 in this volume for a critical discussion of the organisational differences in Rape Crisis Centres). While acknowledging that there are important differences beween individual refuges in terms of all the above characteristics (particularly between those that are part of the Women's Aid Federations and those, the minority, that are not) most commentators would place the UK refuge movement fairly close to this end of the continuum. Both the organisational forms of British refuges and the principles underpinning their work derive from the wider women's movement. In particular, most are committed to non-hierarchical, collectivist ways of working and to the principles of self-help and self-determination. As Kelly argues, refuges offer women not just a place of safety, but also 'a different way of understanding what happened to them and the possibility of not being the "victim" or "client". We talked about self-help, working with women, rather than for them' (1991: 35).

In contrast, American shelters for battered women appear to be further along that continuum towards the more conventional 'social provision' model. Mawby and Gill, for example, argue that their methods reflect a much closer alignment with statutory agencies: '[they] . . . prioritize social-provision goals and make clearer distinctions between helper and helped'(1987: 86). This was not always the case: Tice (1990) describes the radicalism of the early US shelter movement. The first shelters sprang up in the large cities out of existing feminist networks and were run by small-scale collectives committed to mutual self-help and consensual decision-making (Morgan, 1985; Tice, 1990). As in the UK, the shelters formed an essential part of the wider political struggle against the structural oppression of women, emphasising 'The goal of changing the sociopolitical conditions that fostered violence' (Tice, 1990: 85).

Compared to their British counterparts, however, the US shelters' search for funds was much more intensive. Dobash and Dobash write of an 'explosion' of funding in the mid-1970s from private and corporate, as well as local and central state sources (1992). The price paid for financial survival, though, appears to have been high. Funding agencies, particularly federal sources, were often exacting in their requirements. Many argue that in the rush for funds the commitment of shelters to feminist practice was badly compromised (Murray, 1988; Ferraro, 1983; Schecter, 1982).

Two central features of this compromise can be identified. The first involved a break in the essential link between aims and methods: away from the belief – central to the original feminist inspiration – that the way in which help is provided is as important as the help itself. Many shelters moved towards a more traditional relationship between helper and helped and away from collective and democratic decision-making approaches (Wharton, 1987). Hierarchical organisational structures emerged as shelters established boards of directors, management teams and professional staff (Murray, 1988). Power divisions increasingly appeared between different 'ranks' of staff and between staff and women residents (Srinivasan and Davis, 1991; Murray, 1988; Morgan, 1985). By the beginning of the 1980s, many identified a widespread incorporation of the shelters into traditional service bureaucracies (Johnson, 1981; Ferraro, 1983).

The second area of compromise involved the kind of help provided. Part of the shelters' expansion was driven by growing numbers of psycho-medical 'experts' who attached themselves to the shelters and manoeuvred for greater professional ownership and control (Dobash and Dobash, 1987). The result was an increased dominance of the mental health approach which defined the 'problem' as the individual woman and her relationships (Ferraro, 1983; Morgan, 1985). Typically, in this approach the psychological characteristics of the women entering the shelters are assessed in order to determine their suitability for help, while 'treatment' aims to enable them to cope better with their situation (Morgan, 1985). Stress is placed on personal change: women are expected to 'work on themselves' – often over fairly short periods of time – and those who are seen as incapable of changing, or unwilling to change, can be asked to leave (Ferraro, 1983). As Morgan argues: 'Where once the impact of gender domination was raised as a way of understanding violent abuse of women, now the focus is on individual pathology, the 'illness' of the batterer and the psychological profile of the victim' (Morgan, 1985: 66).

As the shelters grew in size their scope also expanded from the provision of individual safe houses to the establishment of more comprehensive 'programmes' involving a wide range of educational and psychotherapeutic services for the whole family (Morgan, 1985; Dobash and Dobash, 1987). Many shelters, particularly those funded by the criminal justice agencies, failed to differentiate between the various constituents of 'family violence': women who had been battered and the men who had battered them were increasingly identified as part of the same 'client group' (Morgan, 1985). Generally then these changes have resulted in a redefinition of the problem from the political and gendered issue of wife assault to the personal and gender-neutral problem of individual or family breakdown. The focus is increasingly on pathological explanations of the problem – on maternal or family 'dysfunction'- and there is a general association of wife battering with other types of 'deviant behaviour', particularly alcohol abuse. The battered wife has become a 'domestic violence program client' (Morgan, 1985).

Clearly, however, these tendencies have not all been one way; there is still optimism that the commitment to feminist practice characterises some parts of the US shelter movement: 'Their spirit of innovation and an ongoing process of defining and specifying feminist practice continues' (Tice, 1990: 85). Davis (1987) argues that although shelters have become increasingly bureaucratic and professionalised, many nevertheless still claim an empowerment philosophy. Others emphasise that the shelter movement remains an area of ongoing political struggle (Murray, 1988; Ahrens, 1980). Moreover, it is important to acknowledge the wide range of different types of shelters in the USA as a result of the sheer size and diversity of the country. Tice (1990), for example, indicates the influence of factors such as geographical location on the work of shelters. Rural shelter groups, for example, have generally been more wary of adopting what could be seen to be confrontational tactics than have those in urban areas. Dobash and Dobash (1992) similarly cite incidences of shelters responding very differently to the same external tendencies.

Against this, however, many argue that the pressures to adopt a non-feminist approach are becoming more and more irresistible. Tierney's (1982) overview of the development of the USA movement concludes that the emergence of traditional service-oriented programmes is likely to continue, under pressure from 'influential sponsors' who seek to deflect the movement away from its more radical agenda. She argues that it is more rather than less likely that in the USA the wife-beating problem will become 'increasingly medicalised, professionalised, individualised and de-politicised' (Tierney, 1982: 216).

The British experience

Money problems

The search for adequate funding has also been an ongoing preoccupation of refuge groups in Britain. Few have ever received the local authority discretionary funding recommended by the 1975 Select Committee on Violence in Marriage. The majority survive on an uncertain combination of short-term grant funding, income from women's rents, and local fund raising. A survey of women's refuges in 1980 revealed that over one-third received no grants at all and that existing sources of funding – then predominantly Urban Aid – were inherently insecure. Only just under one-third were getting any assistance from their local authority. The report concluded that this lack of funding 'seriously curtailed' the work of many groups (Binney *et al.*, 1981).

Problems worsened in the mid-1980s as a result of the changed regulations surrounding the 'board and lodgings payment' to women living in refuges. By removing any allowance for the 'cost of care', the amount available from women's rents to pay for the staff and services provided by refuges was reduced dramatically (Wolmar, 1988). More generally, funding difficulties were exacerbated by tightened central control over local government expenditure. Restrictions were placed both on the non-negotiable sum provided by central government and, as a result of the widespread non-payment of the 'community charge' and its subjection to central government 'capping', on the volume of locally derived revenue. The combined effect was to constrain not only the mainstream activities of local authorities, but also their ability to fund the operation of local community organisations. In 1991 the National Council for Voluntary Organisations, estimated that some £30 million was lost in this way to the voluntary sector (Redding, 1991).

At the end of the decade the government's White Paper *Caring for People* assured the voluntary sector that new funding arrangements would afford it 'a sounder financial base and . . . a greater degree of certainty in planning for the future' (HMSO, 1989: 24). In fact neither occurred. Grants remained time-limited in nature, resulting in a continued log-jam of applications with much of subsequent years' budgets being committed in advance (RTI, 1991). The terms and conditions of available grants were frequently readjusted in line with shifting government priorities – a continuous changing of the funding 'goal posts' – and there was no greater permanence to the grants themselves. Successful agencies were those most able to tack and trim to the changing objectives of government policy. The sheer volume and complexity of the work required to keep abreast of funding shifts placed considerable pressures on underfunded and understaffed organisations. All of which, as Brenton (1985) observed, made for a rather shaky financial basis on which to develop the promised partnership between statutory and non-statutory service providers.

Greater competition

One result of the budgetary difficulties experienced by many local councils was keener pressure on the few additional sources of central government funding that were available.

This encouraged a degree of political opportunism on the part of larger and better resourced groups (Brenton, 1985; Sharron, 1981). As one funding advice body warned its voluntary sector readership, those bidding for central money needed to take an aggressive stance: 'There is already a pecking order, and once that has become firmly re-established you may have missed your chance for some time' (RTI, 1991: 5). In such a climate the members of the traditional 'charity elite' with their high-level political and social connections stood to gain considerable advantage over those not so well connected (Brenton, 1985). In 1991, for example, the National Alliance of Women's Organisations lost nearly two-thirds of its central government grant, while its former 'parent' body, the National Council for Voluntary Organisations retained its £1 million funding (*Observer*, 27 October 1991). Moreover, there was some evidence that at a local level encouragement was being given to established organisations to adopt a 'shop steward' role in respect of the rest of the voluntary sector and collaborate with local authorities in the prioritisation of competing funding bids.[3]

Autonomous women's groups may experience particular difficulties in this increasingly competitive climate due to their uneasy coexistence with the traditional voluntary sector. To survive, many may be forced to seek the support or patronage of more mainstream organisations. Some, for example, may find it necessary to operate under the 'umbrella' of local councils of community or voluntary service, or to link into the special projects work of the centrally favoured local housing associations. While it is clearly important for refuge groups to develop strategic alliances with other groups working within the community, particularly around common issues such as low-cost housing, closer cooperation has its consequences. As much as their statutory counterparts, many established community organisations are characterised by masculinist ways of working and by the continued marginalisation of women's issues. While they may profess a paternalistic concern for the plight of battered wives, most remain resistant to feminist explanations of the problem. In particular they may lack patience or sympathy with the methods of self-help groups; management agreements, for example, may contain requirements about tightening up the group's organisational processes – particularly those of democratic decision-making – and aligning them more closely with the bureaucratic organisational procedures of host organisations.

Greater control

In addition to continued financial insecurity, the activities of voluntary organisations were subject throughout the 1980s to greater political control by local and/or central government (Williams, 1983; Brenton, 1985). In large part this was facilitated by their, albeit reluctant, participation in the new 'contract culture'. The government report entitled *Efficiency Scrutiny on Government Funding of the Voluntary Sector* bemoaned the ad hoc method of voluntary grant aid and recommended greater control of the objectives, methods and outcomes of funded schemes. While there have always been strings on the receipt of such funding, the terms and conditions of government grants were now to be made much more explicit. Increasingly, they were to take the form of agreed contracts with the recipient organisations, establishing concrete, measurable objectives or targets and identifying mechanisms for monitoring and assessing outcomes.

Particularly problematic, especially for groups committed to a feminist practice, was the extent to which the terms and conditions of government grants involved a redefinition of the service problem. In order to attract and maintain funding such groups were, publicly at least, increasingly required to reframe their basic aims and objectives in a more traditional social provision model. Enabling women to achieve self-determina-tion and greater confidence is not the kind of outcome that can be easily quantified and measured. In 1992, for example, the Home Office's 'Grants for Innovative Projects' included the area of 'family violence'. Refuge groups applying for this money found that the government's definition of the problem was not that of the violent male, but the much looser and less gender-specific issue of 'violent families'. Bids were invited for projects concerned with the 'avoidance' and 'treatment' of family violence and implicit in the specifications was the 'cycle of violence' thesis. Successful projects would be those offering 'educational programmes' or the provision of counselling, mediation and help with 'personal problems' (Home Office, *Notes for Guidance*, 1992: *passim*).

While acknowledging the fairly hesitant way in which local authorities, initially at least, embraced the 'contract culture' (Wistow *et al.*, 1992), the growth of contractual agreements between statutory 'purchaser' and non-statutory 'providers' will be an increasing feature of the social care market. At the same time, the financial contraints experienced by statutory agencies will increase the pressure on them to utilise voluntary agencies as substitutes for the services they are no longer able or willing to provide. In this context, there is a strong possibility that the contract mechanism will be used to ensure that voluntary sector providers align their practice more closely with the approaches and methods of the purchasing agency. In this way, many have argued the operation of the contract culture is essentially undermining of the central strength of the voluntary sector: the development of alternative and innovative ways of working (Thornton, 1991). In particular, the development of the purchaser and provider division, with the voluntary and independent sector contracting to supply appropriate packages of care to clients of statutory agencies, may serve to undermine the traditional role of that sector as 'watchdog' or critic of statutory provision. As Drake and Owens point out, there is not a little irony in the proposed juxtaposition of roles: 'the watchdog becoming service provider and the erstwhile service provider . . . becoming the watchdog' (1992: 82).

Refuges and the social work profession

Although social workers have no statutory responsibility for battered women, they nevertheless work closely with the problem. Despite evidence (Maynard, 1985; Borkowski *et al.*, 1983; Leonard and McLeod, 1980) that social workers consistently underestimate the incidence of wife abuse within their caseloads, a study by Binney, Harkell and Nixon in 1981 found that they were the most common source of referral to refuges and their agencies were the second most frequently contacted, after the police, by women seeking help. Generally, however, there has been a rather uneasy relationship between the social work profession and autonomous women's groups such as Women's Aid.

On the one hand, there is evidence of a greater mutual interdependence. For hard-pressed frontline staff, refuges represent a useful resource for women for whom their agencies make no direct provision. In addition, there has been a greater acknowledgement by many social work professionals of the particular skills and expertise held by refuge groups. For those working in refuges, there has in turn been an increased recognition that there are areas of work – such as with women who have alcohol-related or mental health problems – where social workers can offer useful information and advice, as well as access to more specific resources. To an extent, too, there is a greater degree of physical interdependence as social work training courses become more receptive to the idea that refuge work is 'relevant' pre-training experience, and women social workers participate in a personal capacity in refuge groups.

On the other hand, hostility remains within some parts of the social work profession towards the methods and structures of refuge groups – particularly around such issues as access by male social workers and the accommodation of teenage boys – and a scepticism about the ability of refuge staff to deal 'professionally' with issues such as child sexual abuse. This is matched by a continued suspicion on the part of refuge workers about the theoretical approaches underpinning much social work practice, as well as of professionals' unacknowledged appropriation of their skills and knowledge. This mutual wariness has not been much assisted by the fact that feminism remains relatively marginal to the professional curriculum – added on, rather than developed as a central theoretical approach (Hudson, 1989; Carter *et al.*, 1992). This marginality has been exacerbated in more recent years as a result of the more residual role that the Central Council for Education and Training in Social Work (CCETSW) has attempted to accord to social science disciplines more generally (Carter *et al.*, 1992) and as a result of the increased degree of agency control over the content of social work training courses provided for under the new Dip. SW arrangements (Jones, 1989; Parsloe, 1990).

Moreover, central changes in the wider political and ideological context over the 1980s have served to heighten the methodological tensions between the profession and autonomous women's groups. In addition to the more traditional forms of resistance to the theory and practice of feminism – the lingering and ingrained sexism of powerful individuals operating within a masculinist organisational structure – the years of the 1980s have seen the emergence and increasing dominance of a 'post-feminist' approach. In its most reactionary variant, this approach argues that feminism has become an outdated and irrelevant political ideology which fails to comprehend the 'new reality' of the world in which SSDs have to operate. Thus, in the context of child sexual abuse, one principal case worker opined: 'The majority of sexual abuse referrals received by social workers are very different from those relatively few types of cases on which . . . feminists have evolved their perspective, developed their practices and established their reputations.' Feminists, he continues, are locked in sterile and outdated debates and their prejudices and weaknesses 'are potentially harmful to everyone' (O'Hagan, 1989: 13).

The effect of the professional and academic backlash against feminism has been increasingly to squeeze its explanations and analyses from public policy discourse. The excited public debates about child sexual abuse during and following the Cleveland Enquiry of 1987–8, for example, were characterised by the almost complete absence of feminist interpretations, and by the dominance of the views and explanations of male 'experts' (Kelly, 1989b; Campbell, 1988). As Kelly argues, the professionals took central stage: 'We are on occasion credited with having raised the issues, but it is clearly now time for the "real experts" to take over' (1989b: 14). Hudson argues that this process of exclusion is part of a more general wave of 'fury and distortion' against feminism, such that, by the end of the 1980s: 'the idea that feminist perspectives might be "extreme" and "dangerous" had been semi-legitimated in professional social work literature' (1992: 137).

The reaction against feminist theoretical analyses has facilitated the renewed dominance of approaches that individualise the problem of wife beating and ignore its gender determinations. The critique of feminism developed by those like O'Hagan (above) is based largely on the assertion that feminist explanations fail to acknowledge the specificity of each individual occurrence: 'Each act of abuse is unique in the circumstances in which it takes place, the individuals it involves, and its short and long-term impact upon the victim' (1989: 13). Any attempt at wider theoretical understandings are irrelevant, he suggests, to the majority of cases. While it is likely that O'Hagan is relatively extreme in his views, it is clear that the growing tendency of the profession increasingly to restrict its focus to families and individuals considered to be 'at risk' has served more generally to encourage a 'personalising' approach on the part of social workers (McNay, 1992).

Resistance to wider theoretical perspectives inevitably affects both the explanation of the problem and the nature of the social work response. Defined as individual problems they are more likely to be perceived as private problems, largely the responsibility of, and thus within the control of, the individuals or families concerned. Maynard's research on social workers' responses to cases involving wife abuse indicates how they attempted to locate the problem within an essentially privatised notion of 'personal troubles'. The aim of the intervention (or non-intervention) was to restore the equilibrium of the family and of the individuals within it: 'In emphasising that family problems are solvable in individual terms, social work . . . encourages clients to see problems as their problems only and to adapt to their privatised situation' (1985: 138).

Such approaches lead to explanations of the problem in terms of the personal inadequacies of certain kinds of men (or women). From this perspective, of course, they become more tractable to social work intervention. Hence the growth of work with male abusers which tends, with some notable exceptions (see, for example, the work of Jukes (1990) and others) to focus on the personal inadequacies of the men and their need to achieve greater control over their feelings and behaviour. The problem is the extent to which such behaviourist approaches, in conjunction with an emphasis on social factors such as poverty, stress and unemployment, make the violent response of the individual male at the least 'understandable' and, at the worst, to some extent 'excusable'. The fact that many women experience these pressures and do not resort to violence, and that many men who batter their wives and partners do not experience them, may be ignored (Maguire, 1988). While such approaches may have some impact on the violence of an individual male (although the evidence suggests that the cessation of violent behaviour is typically short-term), it does nothing to confront the larger problem of men's abusive power over women. It is particularly problematic to the extent that it is perceived by the aggressor as an (easy) alternative to sentencing, or if resources are put into this area of work at the expense of funding for work with women who have been battered (Jukes, 1990; Horley, 1990b).

There are similar problems with the general 'degenderising' of the issue that results. Public and media debates about child sexual abuse in the 1980s, for example, were increasingly dominated by a 'sex-blind' approach. Thus Pizzey, in a letter to *The Independent*, argued the need to 'put aside the assumption that all issues of abuse are issues of gender' (7 July 1990). On the one hand, this approach serves to obscure the fact that, in the great majority of cases, abuse occurs at the hands of men. On the other hand, it results in disproportionate public attention being paid to the relatively few occurrences of female child abusers (Driver and Droisen, 1989). In the same way, in the area of wife assault, we have the emergence of the 'battered husband syndrome'. This is particularly associated with the work of Straus *et al.* (1980) in the USA, who argued that 'The most unreported crime is not now wife beating – it's husband beating.' The result has been a growth in calls for 'refuges for men' in both the USA and the UK, despite evidence that in the majority of such cases women resorted to violence as a (largely ineffectual) means of self-defence (Saunders, 1988). As Saunders concludes: '. . . to label self-defense husband abuse serves to direct attention away from the victimisation of the woman and the function of male dominance' (1988: 90).

The expansion of Victim Support Schemes (VSS) into the area of 'family violence' may be a good example of the operation of both these central tendencies: the individualisation and degenderisation of the problem. The concept of 'victim' is essentially individual and sexless – a 'catch-all' category that fails to differentiate between such qualitatively different experiences as, say, theft and rape. Whether or not, as some have argued (Maguire, 1988), the growth of VSS is a deliberate attempt to circumvent the work of feminist-inspired groups in the area of rape and wife assault, at the very least it is likely that, in a context of competitive funding, the expansion of VSS into areas presently well served by autonomous women's groups may result in the diversion of resources away from those groups (see Chapter 1 in this volume).

Negotiating the pressures

Some of the demands and tensions of their changed financial and political context can be managed fairly easily by refuge groups. Such groups have always engaged in a degree of compromise and negotiation for the greater good of the women in the house or the longer-term future of the refuge. Many, for example, may establish separate organisational structures, with representatives from statutory agencies, in order to respond to the formal liaison requirements of funding agencies. These public meetings may have little real impact on the day-to-day running of the refuge. In such ways, it may be possible to play the funding game with few actual consequences for the refuges' basic principles of operation. Years of co-working at 'grassroots' level, moreover, may have established reasonable working arrangements between individual refuge groups and staff of funding agencies such as housing and social services. At the very least, the valuable resource represented by refuge provision may have secured a (albeit possibly temporary) resignation on the part of other voluntary and statutory agencies to their perceived 'idiosyncratic' ways of working.

In many cases, however, there will be requirements that bite deeper into the basic principles of the refuge movement. Such is the demand made by some social services departments that refuges only offer places to women with children, or that refuge child care workers are paid scales consistent with that agency's low valuation of the work involved. Involvement of representatives of local housing agencies may result in greater scrutiny of refuges' compliance with the overcrowding regulations, causing considerable tension with their 'open door' policies. The funding of paid staff within the refuge is another potential area of difficulty, as unpaid volunteers are required to manage the employment of their colleagues and monitor their performance on behalf of the funding agency. In turn, divisions may emerge within the collective as paid workers join trades unions in order to protect or enhance the terms and conditions of their employment. Generally, the existence of external funding increases the amount of public scrutiny over the operation of refuges, the practices of those who work with them, and the lives of those who live within them. Simply to survive, many refuge groups may be increasingly forced in the longer term to 'trade off' basic operational principles for a series of shorter-term gains.

One key difference between the British refuge movement and its American counterpart, however, relates to the nature and influence of its organisational and political base. In the USA, feminism was only one ideological inspiration among others for the shelter movement. Equally important were the civil rights and legal advocacy approach and what Tierney (1982) has called the 'community mental health ideology'. Most importantly, while these various inspirations fed the movement in slightly different ways, there was no central umbrella organisation to coordinate and consolidate the movement's key operational principles. As Tierney argues, this has resulted in the movement developing a wide range of strategies and approaches. While this may enhance the flexibility of individual shelters to adapt to local conditions and funding requirements (Judkins, 1989), it also increases the vulnerability of those shelters to local 'sponsor preference' and weakens the possibility of a collective resistance to the factors undermining their feminist practice.

In the UK the majority of local groups are affiliated to one of the Women's Aid Federations of England, Scotland, Wales or Northern Ireland. While assuring the member groups' autonomy at a local level, the function of these umbrella organisations is to promote the interests and concerns of local groups at a national level, and to campaign for the wider socio-legal changes necessary to improve the plight of battered women. The goals and practice of the Federations derive explicitly from those of the wider women's movement; while the characteristics of individual refuges may vary considerably, affiliation requires that all member groups subscribe to a broadly feminist approach. The progress of the Federations has not been smooth; the English Federation, in particular, has been characterised by major political divisions. As Kelly argues, the Federations represent both a 'source of strength and an area of ongoing tension' (1991: 33). The tension has derived from their function as a crucible for intense internal debates about the theory and practice of the refuge movement. Their great strength, however, has been precisely to perform such a function and in so doing to enable the constituent groups to retain a sense of collective struggle and purpose.

Conclusion

Its relative success in attracting funding appears to have exacted some major compromises from the American shelter movement. The increased bureaucratisation of shelters and the greater professional 'colonisation' of the problem seems in many cases to have diverted the shelters' original feminist inspiration into a less radical form of service provision. This chapter has argued that some of the pressures and tensions affecting the development of the American movement may be increasingly experienced by its British counterpart. In particular, the greater competition for funding, and the enhanced degree of political control over the terms and conditions of that funding, may be forcing refuge groups into more traditional methods and practices. The general political backlash against feminism, moreover, has resulted in the renewed dominance of individualising and gender-neutral explanations of the problem within both public and professional debates. The rise of VSS and its expansion into the area of wife assault may be offering local and central government a cheaper and more politically acquiescent alternative to feminist-inspired women's groups.

However, it has been argued that individual refuge groups have managed in varying ways to negotiate or resist many of these pressures to change and that the existence of the Women's Aid Federations has been important in this process. In the new political and financial climate within which individual refuge groups now have to work, it is likely that the role of the Federations will become even more vital. New strategies for survival may need to be developed at a national as well as at a local level, if the operation of refuges as feminist practice is to be protected. Current national work on the development of good practice guidelines around such issues as funding criteria, equal opportunities, employment of paid staff, childcare work and so on, for example, may enable individual groups to operate effectively within the new contract culture with minimal compromise to their more basic principles. Against this, however, we must place the enormity of the changes that have reworked the face of public sector services over the last decade, and the sheer strength of the ideological backlash against feminism. Even with the backing of the Federations, it will be a difficult task for refuges individually or collectively to resist the various pressures for change. The degree of recognition and support provided by their colleagues in the voluntary sector and by the many professionals who use their services will be a key factor in their ultimate survival as a distinctive form of feminist-inspired practice.

Notes

1. See the Introduction in this volume for an explanation of the use of the term 'wife' in this context.
2. See Dobash and Dobash (1987 and 1992) for a comparative discussion of the origins and development of the UK and USA refuge movements.
3. One example of this is known to the author. In 1990 one local authority invited representatives of the local Council of

Community Service and one of the city's largest Housing Associations to assist it in prioritising the 'top ten' bids for funding following severe cutbacks in its grants to voluntary organisations. The local refuge group's bid for continued funding of two workers was effectively deprioritised and out of the running for funding until word leaked out about this essentially private process. A subsequent appeal was successfully made, part of which argued against any attempt to 'divide and rule' between groups whose services are effectively interdependent.

4

Asian Women and Violence from Male Partners

Kish Bhatti-Sinclair

Introduction

This chapter will focus on the ways in which Asian[1] women perceive themselves, their families, their relationships with men, and the violence they experience. Attention will be paid to the particular nature of the oppression these women suffer in the context of a range of other structural disadvantages: inadequate housing, poor health care, language and religious barriers and, most of all, lack of access to public services. The chapter will also examine the response of Asian communities to the issue of violence against women and consider the extent to which the nature of their response makes it easier for statutory and non-statutory agencies to ignore the problem.

Examination of the literature reveals relatively little published material on the issue of black[2] women generally, and even less on the subject of violence within the home. This contrasts with the wide body of work on white women suffering abuse from partners (Hanmer and Maynard, 1987; Borkowski et al., 1983; Wilson, 1983; Hanmer and Saunders, 1984; Dobash and Dobash, 1980). Little reference is made to the experience of black women within these works, and that which is made is considered by some black women to be marginalising and dismissive. Most importantly, such literature typically ignores the most critical factor in the lives of black women living in Britain today: racism.

The literature confirms that there are different issues affecting the experiences of black and white women. For example, whereas some white feminists have identified the family as the source of women's oppression, Asian women continue to look to the family for economic security, the setting of standards on acceptable behaviour, the resolution of conflict and, above all, the provision of support and shelter. Radical white feminism is open to criticism by black women in so far as it develops a race-blind approach that fails to take into account issues fundamental to black women, such as the role of the family:

> A key source of counter-attack to the feminist critique of the family has come from black feminists who have vocalized their defence of the black family-household as an arena of solidarity and resistance against racism in both Britain and the USA (Tang Nain, 1991: 9).

The value of the work on white women and wife assault is immeasurable in so far as exploration is needed of how class and gender act as oppressive factors on women's lives. Further attention, however, must be paid to the acquisition of more in-depth knowledge of the experiences of black women, both in terms of the violence they suffer and their treatment at the hands of the 'helping' agencies. Practitioners need to become aware of the limitations of race-blind service delivery and of the moral and legal imperative to develop and implement practices that offer an equitable service to black women (Dominelli, 1988; Ahmed, 1990; Mama, 1989a).

The research on which this chapter is based was undertaken to give voice to the struggles of a small number of Asian women living in Britain today and to add to the knowledge about black women's experience of violence from partners. The study took place over a six-month period and developed a qualitative rather than quantitative methodology. Potential respondents were identified through personal or work contacts: referrals from agencies such as Women's Aid, housing and social services and local community activists. Some women acted as 'go-betweens' because they felt sufficiently inflamed by the issue, and this gave them an opportunity to contribute and support their women friends and relatives. In-depth interviews were undertaken personally by the researcher. No interpreters were used as the presence of a third (unknown) person would have changed the dynamics of the interview. Occasionally, another trusted professional or friend was present.

To succeed, the researcher had to gain the confidence of the women interviewed, and establish a meaningful relationship with them. Frequently, this involved more than one meeting. Each meeting lasted between two to three hours. Follow-up work was also undertaken with approximately half of the interviewees. The method chosen required a certain amount of emotional input on the part of the interviewer and the use of sensitively adapted counselling skills. Many women interviewed found the process of re-living their experiences extremely painful. Often the first hour was spent in angry outpourings, as this was often the first time they had spoken to anyone about their suffering. Many had not even spoken to their own parents or family for fear of creating additional anguish.

Knowledge of the local communities and Asian languages was an important prerequisite of the study. The interviews were conducted in the language with which the interviewee was most comfortable: Punjabi, Hindi and Urdu were the most frequently used. A few women were happier communicating in English. Confidentiality had to be guaranteed to all the women, as they did not want to be exposed to criticism from the communities in which they lived and worked. This was maintained with increasing difficulty as the researcher was sometimes in touch with several women in the same family at the same time. What follows is the experience of the twenty women interviewed, reproduced as far as possible in their own words. In the interests of confidentiality, the names of those speaking have been changed.

Nature and duration of violence

All the women had suffered sustained physical and mental abuse over periods lasting between ten and sixteen years. Few had approached any outside agency for help in the initial years of suffering, a finding substantiated by Mama (1989b). When interviewed, eleven women were living away from their husbands, five were still living with their partners, two were living in the same property but were effectively separated, and two were widowed and living in their own house/flat with their mothers-in-law. The majority had received some help with their housing needs, particularly from a local housing association that had strong links with black people. Six were living in properties owned by the housing association, two were living in council-owned accommodation, two were in the Women's Refuge, six were living with either family or friends and four were living in owner-occupied accommodation.

Many women reported severe physical or mental abuse from the very start of their marriages. Sushma married young:

> The beatings started early, he would hit me if I questioned him on anything, one time he threw my exercise bike at me. He would come home drunk and sit on me and beat me; because of him I had two miscarriages.

Amritpal was married for two years: her experience demonstrates that dowry demands were only part of the problem:

> I spent quite a few hours with him and was asked if I wanted to marry him, our families knew each other well. I liked what I saw of him and I agreed. At first it was okay. Then he said that what my family had given as a dowry was not enough, and his parents agreed. Then they started to treat me badly. I had by then started to work in the family business. When I began, there were five workers, but slowly they got rid of the other workers. In the end I was running the place on my own. I worked all day, then at night I went home and did all the housework. I was never given any

money or wages. I had no time to rest. He stopped talking to me.
He would hit me.

Amritpal's experience of progressively worsening violence is a
common one. In addition, she was being exploited as an
unpaid labourer, an issue further explored by Parmar (1982).

Violence within domestic settings affects all socio-economic
groups and in our study there were women who could survive
independently. This is true of Amritpal, who studied for her
B. A. degree in India before coming to live with her husband's
family:

> They were quite rich, their house is big and luxurious but it was
> miles from anywhere. I found life there very difficult. He went out
> himself a lot and came back late at night and never said how he
> spent his time.

In the majority of Asian religions (particularly Islam)
alcohol is forbidden, a taboo subject. Alcohol abuse can
therefore be ignored, and women may feel reluctant to discuss
the problem within their community. Alcohol and other
addictions, however, were an important factor in the lives of
at least eight of the women. The husbands of two respondents
died relatively young of alcohol-related illnesses. Tara was one
such example:

> Two years ago, after eleven years of marriage, I went to my
> solicitor and started divorce proceedings. I was again living in
> bed/breakfast accommodation. By now my husband was drinking
> too much and because he suffered with a heart problem he died
> just two weeks before the divorce came through . . . my mother-
> in-law still blames me for his death. But she lives near me and I
> look after her because her health is not good.

A significant number of women reported that their marriage
was harmed by their husbands' affairs with other women.
Parminder's husband controlled her completely, while maintaining a relationship with another woman:

Very soon after I joined him in England I realised that he had a white girlfriend. He started giving me a bad time, he would hit me and go away and stay with her. He would leave me alone a lot at night. I wasn't allowed to go out at all, not even to the shops – he would come and do all the shopping. He didn't like me to make friends. We moved from the area where most Asian people live to a place where there are very few people from our community, so I haven't made any friends at all. I have no family of my own in this country. I have no one.

Shakeela also suffered as a result of her husband's relationship with another woman:

I married because my parents wished it; I had no say. I was married for over seven years. Early on it was better because he didn't drink and he didn't have a girlfriend. Then he started to come and go as he pleased. If I stopped him from going to see his girlfriend or from drinking, he would hit me. Twice he kicked me in the head with his steel-tipped toes and split my head open.

The available choices

Seven of the women were still living in the same house as their husbands. The majority stated lack of knowledge of alternatives and relevant provision as reasons for remaining, but lack of self-esteem and confidence are also important factors. Many women, however, regardless of where they were brought up, expressed a long-term commitment to their marriages. This was true even for those no longer living with their partners. As Gifford argues: 'To most Asian women, the thought of life outside the structure of marriage and family is not a desirable one' (1990: 155).

The strong desire to see their marriage work was true of many respondents. When asked why she stays, Rekha explained:

He might change if we have our own place. When the baby arrives he'll be different because of the child and I think that a child needs a father.

Similarly, Sara does not feel she can act yet, despite having been abused for fourteen years:

I'll spend the next years as I've spent the last fourteen. I don't intend to do anything until he pushes me too far.

Family and friends

A high percentage of interviewees had sought help from family and friends as the first port of call. Unfortunately, many Asian women in Britain lack the support systems available to them in their country of origin:

Traditionally, an Indian wife is not supposed to defend herself verbally to her husband and her in-laws. Back home in India, when marriage fails, the process that would be put into operation would involve one's closest family and friends. Social pressures would not allow a woman to set foot outside her home (Shan, 1985: preface).

Smitta was married for ten years and, fortunately, received all the help she needed from her family:

Through all that time I kept trying to leave him. Every time I would go to my parents' home and every time he would bring elders of the community and relatives to our house. They told my parents that this is the way it is and that I would have to put up with it. They told my mother to keep out of it. But I was lucky, because my mother stuck by me. I don't know what I would have done without her.

Smitta is now divorced and living on her own with her children. As is Kalwant whose parents, unusually, also live in the same city as her:

Out of the ten years of our marriage, I only stayed four with my husband. It helped a lot having my parents so close, I would have gone bonkers if they hadn't helped me.

Supportive family and friends can make all the difference to the choices available to women. When Salma's husband became violent, her family tried to help her:

After two years I became desperate – I couldn't go on. Once he beat me so much I was unconscious for three or four hours. I called all my relatives together and told them that I was going to leave him. My dad agreed that I had tried hard to make the marriage work.

Others saw the family itself as part of the problem. Yasmin's marriage lasted two years. She feels devastated by the fact that she is still so young but already separated from her husband, and feels her family is to blame:

Parents are responsible. I was too inexperienced to make the right choices. If young people do express opinions, they are ignored because they are inexperienced. I was married when I was eighteen. Girls should get married when they are older. There isn't enough investigation into the families or the men.

Many respondents felt that Asian women are not equipped to deal with life outside their family homes. The support provided by nuclear and extended families is difficult to reproduce in an alien environment. As Gifford argues:

Our psyche and needs are different. We perhaps do want to get in the kitchen and cook curry, we perhaps do want to wear the *salwar kamiz*, we perhaps do want to go to Indian movies and watch something romantic, we do want to be with babies because we were brought up with them. I don't know any Asian who wasn't and that is part of our 'Indianness' (1990: 155).

The community

Families can themselves face difficulties in supporting their daughters. They can also feel trapped by the situation. Custom dictates that they have handed over responsibility for their daughters, so they may face community derision for 'interfering' in marital relationships. Some families are not even aware that a problem exists. The lack of support from the local communities, coupled with almost total control over them by their husbands, made for a prisoner-like existence for some of the women. Withdrawal of basic rights was reported again and again. Although not physically kept prisoner in her home, Parminder felt trapped by the power her husband wielded over her:

> He kept hold of my passport and would send me away to India for long periods. The last time he sent me to India, I realised that while I was there my passport had expired, so it took me months longer to get back to Britain.

With no family of her own in Britain, Sara was very dependent on her husband; she did not feel able to go to others in her community for help:

> He won't stop drinking. He doesn't care if I stay or leave. No one in our community knows. There's no one I can turn to for help. I would prefer to go to someone outside of my community for help but, before I spoke to you, I didn't know where I could go for help. I would like to go to people who understand me – who would help me to cope. I don't know about the world out there – I don't know how I would get on.

In some cases, the women in our study had suffered abuse from other members of their husband's family:

> In those days my mother-in-law had a drink problem as well as my husband. Between them they used to keep me in the house. I

wasn't allowed to see anyone or telephone anyone. Not even Mum and Dad.

A number of the women interviewed said that the wider community had very little knowledge of the situation they were in. As a result, they felt that their needs had been largely ignored. All agreed that the issue of wife assault should be more openly discussed within their communities. Professional women workers have found it difficult to raise the issue not only within the community itself, but also with relevant agencies, for fear of alienating families in the area. As a result, many agencies have in effect colluded with the aggressors by ignoring the needs of battered women.

The professionals

Legal

Contact with the legal profession had not proved fruitful for many Asian women, some of whom found the public display of their personal lives extremely difficult. Smitta explains:

> When we eventually went to Court for the divorce, I felt terribly embarrassed. I wished I didn't have to be there. Because the men from his family were there, I had to cover my face.

Many reported that they left their homes without their belongings and the court systems did not move quickly or efficiently enough for the recovery of sometimes expensive jewellery and clothing. As Gita discovered:

> When I went to the solicitor, I asked for all my belongings back but I didn't specify the presents which I received at the wedding. So I didn't get my presents or my jewellery back. I wish my solicitor had had more experience in doing this kind of work. I went to her for advice. I expected her to know what she was doing.

A number of women interviewed were vociferous in their condemnation of the treatment meted out to their friends and relatives, and felt that the law should be changed. A relation of Amritpal's displayed extreme anger:

> They come along and ruin a girl's life and we have no comeback. There should be a law against it. Laws are the only way things will change.

Health services

The effect of sustained physical and mental abuse on women has been considered in detail in a number of studies (Dobash and Dobash, 1980; Borkowski, Murch and Walker, 1983; Hanmer and Maynard, 1987). The on-going torture through which women live daily not only harms them physically, but may also cause them long-term psychological damage. Many women in our study reported that they were suffering from some form of depression and lack of self-confidence. Two women had received long-term psychiatric treatment. Some of the women talked of suicide as a way out. Amritpal became increasingly desperate as her husband tightened his physical control over her:

> He vetted the letters from my parents. If he didn't like them he would tear them up. I wasn't allowed to watch television. He often went out by himself and didn't come back until the early hours of the morning. He never told me how he spent his time – he said it was nothing to do with me. I was so lonely – I tried to kill myself.

Outside the family, there are two agencies with which most women with children have natural contacts. The first is the school and the second is the health service. Contact with either appears legitimate to husbands and families. Many women reported that the first outside contacts they had were with their GPs. Tara suffered for many years before she saw a doctor:

> When I fell pregnant with my older child, he was still knocking me around. He stopped me from seeing my doctor, but one day I was so ill, I managed to drag myself to a neighbour's door and she took me to see a doctor and then I was sent to the hospital. When I got there, I told the hospital social worker. Because I was not eating, I was kept in the hospital for a long time. My child was only two weeks early, but weighed only two pounds.

Doctors and health visitors are also in a unique position because they are seen as acceptable visitors to women's homes and are able to offer face-to-face confidential advice and information. Medical professionals, however, do not always offer the access to services that should be available to women by right. Discriminatory practice may give rise to serious health inequalities (Brent CHC, 1981; Swarup, 1992).

In particular, many health professionals advise battered women to return to their families. Laxsmi has been married for a number of years and still lives in the same house as her violent husband. She has been admitted to psychiatric hospital on several occasions:

> The last time I was there, they told me there was nothing more they could do for me – they closed my case. They said that it was a family problem and that the family should sort it out. It was a waste of time going there anyway because they pumped me full of drugs so much that I put on lots of weight and walked about like a zombie.

Rekha lives with her husband's family in poor-quality accommodation. Her husband continued to beat her through-out her pregnancy:

> There's no wallpaper on the walls, just bare plaster. We've had no hot water for three or four years. We don't have a washing machine so I have to wash everybody's clothes by hand. It's hard

living with his family. When I went to the doctor and told him, he said I should leave my husband and go back to my parents.

Rekha lost her baby in the first week after giving birth.

Professionals working with Asian women need to be aware that returning to the parental home may be an unacceptable step. Women do not want their personal 'failure' to tarnish the reputation of their families. Furthermore, the advice to return home hardly provides the basis for women to make informed and intelligent choices. Instead, it may leave women with the impression that there is in fact no choice at all.

Personal social services

In recent years there has been a growth of literature on social work with black families (Ahmed, Cheetham and Small, 1986; Dominelli, 1988). Much of this is critical of social work practice and of the lack of real provision for black people by social services departments (Swarup, 1992). Ahmed asserts that much social work practice still marginalises the experience of black people:

> In social work, there is a tendency to keep social work with Black families outside the mainstream framework of social work theory and practice. Perception and assumption that perpetuate this tendency usually stem from the notion that 'special' needs of Black families are so alien that they cannot relate to mainstream social work (1990: 4).

The experiences recounted in this study confirm such a view. Twelve of the women interviewed were parents, the majority with children under eight years of age. Some of these children were 'at risk' as the families involved were living on low incomes with inadequate housing and no access to appropriate facilities. As this is the criterion for social services' involvement, it can be a crucial way into potential help for battered women. Salma went to the Department for help when her daughter began to show signs of anxiety:

My daughter was terrified that her dad would beat us up in the street. I wanted their help, but the only thing they came up with was a project, which is all-white, for parents and children under five.

Social workers can play a critical role in enabling women to take control of their lives. Conversely, they also possess the power not only to shake women's confidence, but effectively to take away the very reason many want to survive. Sushma was married for ten years. After giving birth to her third child she suffered from postnatal depression:

> I was on special pills, they made me feel awful. I felt dopey all the time. In that state I didn't know whether I was coming or going. One day my husband made me sign papers, I didn't know what they were. I later realised that I had signed over the right to keep my children with me. He took the kids and moved away. I had no idea where to go. It took me eighteen months to find them. I had no help from Social Services at all. Eventually I managed to gain fortnightly access for three months. After three months I was called to a Social Services office in the West Midlands where my children were asked by social workers in front of me whether they would like to see me regularly. My small children were withdrawn and quiet, but my eldest gave them the impression that he would be happy if I didn't continue with the access.

At a subsequent court appearance, Sushma's request for custody and access was rejected. Her history of depression and the children's lack of enthusiasm were given as reasons for the withdrawal of her rights to see her children.

The majority of the women had no knowledge of the work of the social services department and many did not use social workers because of these professionals' scant knowledge of black communities. It was felt that many lacked the expertise that would enable them to work effectively with these communities. As Ahmed (1990) indicates, however, some progress has been made in recent years. In particular, both the 1989 Children Act and the 1990 NHS and Community Care

Act made specific (albeit brief) mention of the importance of identifying the service needs of local black communities. As she argues:

> This is both encouraging and welcoming. Social workers must grab this as an opportunity to steer ahead and make maximum use of Black communities as a resource for change.

Housing services

Much work has been published on the responses of local authorities to the issue of wife assault (Carew-Jones and Watson, 1985; Wilson, 1983; Hanmer and Saunders, 1984; Edwards, 1989). Several studies have also focused specifically on the needs of black women and how racism has affected their access to services (Bryan, Dadzie and Scafe, 1985; Mama, 1989b). While there is a statutory obligation on local authority housing departments to recognise the needs of those who have accommodation, but are unable to live there, individual responses vary from department to department (Mama, 1989b).

Many women found access to housing services still restricted to decentralised offices where Asian women workers were employed as main-grade workers. Very few visited the central Housing Aid office where the processing of all homelessness cases takes place. While some authorities make interpretation and translation services available, this is useful only in so far as the rest of the system is in place. Parminder was able to discover her way around the agencies with the help of an interpreter working with Women's Aid:

> . . . I knew I had to do something. With the help of the Refuge workers, who called in interpreters, I began to understand what I had to do. I managed to persuade my husband to go to the Housing Department so that he could have our Council house placed in my name only. It was in both our names at the time, he thought that he was going to have it solely placed in his name. We

were interviewed by an Asian woman – when I tried to speak, my husband told me to be quiet in my language. The woman heard him and spoke to us in our language. My husband was so shocked that he signed the house over to me and left the office. The woman later visited me at home and reassured me that I was not alone in this situation. I found her very helpful.

The police

The issue of law enforcement within black communities is a highly controversial one. Negative stereotyping of black people individually and within family groups is pervasive (Bryan, Dadzie and Scafe, 1985). In particular, Asian women are perceived as passive, and the Asian family well able to deal with 'domestic' problems within its own community (Edwards, 1989). Half of those interviewed had called the police at some point in their relationship. Smitta called them only once or twice and found them to be less than sympathetic. She was told:

'You Indian people are all the same, the women never say anything if we take it further.' They always wanted proof of injury and much of what I suffered wasn't physical.

Salma also called the police on one occasion and was equally disillusioned when they told her:

'Unless you've got a bruise, there's nothing we can do about it. Perhaps you should lock yourself up in a room.'

The police clearly did not understand how brave a step it was for some women to go to them, sometimes against the wishes of their families, and one that was often taken only after many years of ill-treatment. For many it was the first step towards gaining control of their lives; an admission of the failure not only of their marriage, but of the traditional way of life that they held dear.

Some women did find the police response more positive, but then found the next steps a little more difficult. Tara left her husband with two small children in tow:

> That particular time that I left him I went to the police and they were good but I had to stay in a police cell with my children for three days. We slept on a single bed. It was terrible. Eventually they found me a bed and breakfast place.

Women's Aid

The local Women's Aid group runs a refuge in the city staffed and managed by white women, with the exception of two Asian women volunteers. A slow trickle of black women has used the refuge partly as a result of lack of alternative provision. Seven out of the twenty women interviewed had stayed in a refuge at some time, not all locally. Three of these had experienced some form of racism from white women in the refuge. Interestingly, they appeared to attribute little significance to the incidents, accepting them perhaps as par for the course. Salma was referred to the refuge by the local housing department:

> I stayed at the refuge for about a month. The workers there were really helpful with food, taxis and solicitors. I got on with most of the women there. Once or twice I heard the words 'paki' and 'you smell'. But I felt happy about leaving my child in the care of the women there.

As with many such projects, the local refuge suffers from shortage of staff and resources. Its priority is work with the women and children. Developmental and educational work with outside bodies has to be done in any spare time. In addition to reduced resources, its workers are experiencing greater difficulties supporting women through the courts. There is increasing pressure on workers to encourage women in considerable distress to have their injuries documented by the police, doctors or solicitors.

Lack of commitment by the authorities means that the refuge building is overcrowded and without space for a separate room that could be made available for the use of Asian women. Cultural and religious needs such as privacy, a place for prayer and special cooking facilities, have not been given the necessary priority. All the women interviewed who used the refuge felt let down by the lack of facilities appropriate to their needs. Parminder went with her children out of desperation:

> Whilst I was there I was very upset. I couldn't understand the ways of the other women living there. One of the white women was messing around with boyfriends. There were drinks and cigarettes. If anyone from my community or family had seen the people I was living with, I would have been tarnished with the same brush. When I was there, I did get help and advice from another Asian woman who was living there. No one else spoke my language. The workers helped as best they could. I only spent a few nights there. We need somewhere where our ways will be understood and respected.

Conclusion

Clearly, the information presented in this study is limited. There are many areas of concern that have not been touched on which may benefit from further study. For example, the extent to which violence within the home affects children and young people, the power relationships between women related by marriage (mothers and sisters-in-law) and the degree of collusion that sometimes exists between the perpetrators and service providers. Attention also needs to be paid more generally to the effects of policing practice and immigration legislation on the lives of Asian women.

However, many important issues have been aired and some conclusions can be reached. Much of the evidence reinforces the findings of Mama (1989a) on the degree and extent of violence suffered by women, the effects of racism on the family, the discriminatory practices of statutory and non-statutory agencies, and so on. The interview data suggest that key services are not available to black women as they are to the rest of society. It also seems that very few agencies are truly committed to providing the resources that could increase access to those services. These findings are reinforced by Swarup's larger-scale study (1992).

While those agencies actively implementing anti-discriminatory practices are closer to equalising access, the best work is being done by black workers employed in positions of some authority. As information on services to black people becomes more widely available, it is clear that black people themselves are in the best position to develop effective services for their communities. Nationally, all projects for black women have been initiated and run by black women and the issue of black women's powerlessness has been raised at the political level primarily by black women.

Recommendations

It is clear that relevant agencies have a moral and legal duty to respond more effectively to the needs of black women. All statutory and non-statutory agencies need to evaluate their methods of delivering services and ensure that gaps are identified and filled as appropriate. Multi-agency responses both locally and nationally are essential to the development of effective policies and guidelines on wife abuse. Consultation should be sought with black women's groups, more black women need to be employed in responsible jobs and equal-opportunities units should be established and/or advisers appointed.

Local authorities

Social service departments must appoint advisers; consult extensively with their local communities; offer concrete resources; train all white staff to challenge racism; offer black staff opportunities to acquire status and support them fully against anti-discriminatory practice.

The processes for making grants to voluntary organisations should be made more accessible to women's groups generally; black advisers would be better at making links and supporting Asian women through the funding maze. As grant aid is given primarily to white organisations, it is crucial that good equal-opportunities practice is insisted upon by grant givers.

The development of interpreting and translation services should be prioritised. Not only can they make life easier for people whose first language is not English, but they would also offer social services and other agencies a more effective way of working through what are often complicated cases – for example, in child protection.

Training courses for people working in the caring professions such as health and housing workers, police officers and teachers should encompass race as an integral part of the course. The social work validating body CCETSW is currently evaluating the race element on all social work courses. This is a good example of a national move having a local impact. Despite this, there are still social work courses throughout the country that are lagging behind in the implementation of good anti-racist practice.

Education departments need to appoint specialist advisers to make an input into the school- and youth-service curricula on issues such as wife abuse.

Voluntary organisations

Voluntary organisations, such as housing associations, play an important role in the lives of many battered women seeking alternative accommodation. In the locality of this study, however, only one special-needs project, funded by the Housing Corporation, exists for battered women.

Several national studies have concluded that Asian women must have easy access to safe emergency housing set up exclusively for them. (Ahmed, Cheetham and Small, 1986; Mama, 1989a, b; Scottish Women's Aid, n.d.). This study has reinforced this view. Local authorities play a critical role in the development of such provision as they alone can provide the longer-term security of funding.

Women's refuges have to examine their methods of work and build on current good practice. Staff training and recruitment practices have to change if black women are to play an equal part in the refuge movement. Separate refuges for black women should not mean that white women can abdicate responsibility and yet again push the issue to one side. Advice and support must be sought from Asian women's groups and Asian women residents if real change is to occur.

Generic counselling services such as the Samaritans and Relate should consider carefully the extent to which their services are fully accessible to black women. They will need to develop appropriate policies and guidelines for training white staff and for recruiting black volunteers.

Notes

1. The term 'Asian' is used in the context of this chapter to describe women who originate from the Indian sub-continent (i.e. India, Pakistan, Bangladesh or Africa). It does not necessarily depict their place of birth or nationality.
2. The term 'black' is used as a political term for people who suffer from racism and powerlessness. This term is used in the text where the discussion does not refer solely to the situation of Asian women. Neither term is ideal, and does not portray the full variety of backgrounds and experiences involved. However, the terms have been used for the sake of brevity.

5

Social Work with Mothers whose Children have been Sexually Abused

Claudia Bernard

Introduction

In this chapter I propose to examine the particular obstacles facing practitioners who attempt to utilise feminist theory in work with women whose children have been sexually abused by their male partners. The central theme of my discussion will be the way practitioners incorporate feminist theory into their practice as a challenge to stereotypical views of the family, particularly women's role in the family. I will assess the extent to which, and the conditions under which, such incorporation is possible. Consideration will also be given to the values underpinning the process of practice, and particular attention will be paid to the notion of a value-free practice. Data from a small-scale study conducted with professionally qualified and experienced social work practitioners working in a local authority setting will be used as illustration throughout the text.[1]

Confronting myths and challenging oppression

Social work practice in the area of child sexual abuse presents practitioners with a major challenge. Of all the issues they have to deal with, child sexual abuse involves the greatest dilemmas for individual practitioners. It is, by its very nature, a distressing and disturbing subject that raises strong emotions in all of us. Feelings and ideas about mothers are one of the most difficult and controversial aspects of the work (MacLeod and Saraga, 1988a). Those attempting to apply feminist knowledge to this area of practice are faced with particular challenges. When we look at the multi-faceted issues that surround sexual abuse, the complexities of gender dynamics and power are highlighted. In particular, there is the dominant familial ideology that promotes the ideal of the family as a heterosexual, two-parent, middle-class unit (Barratt and McIntosh, 1982). Social workers have to deal not only with these factors, but also with the adverse publicity and criticism levelled at them for having too much power over the private sphere of the family. All these factors inextricably link to make the task of the practitioner an arduous one (Masson and O'Byrne, 1990).

From the 1980s onwards we have witnessed a proliferation of sexual abuse cases coming to public attention, as well as being reported to statutory agencies. This has been a result partly of the efforts of the women's movement, but also because of adult survivors 'breaking the silence' (Hall and Lloyd, 1989). While it is difficult to estimate the true incidence of child sexual abuse, as much of it remains hidden, recent evidence suggests that it is more prevalent than was previously thought (Kelly, Regan, and Burton, 1991). A range of theoretical perspectives has been put forward to explain child sexual abuse. At one end of the range are those that locate the problem within individual and family dynamics (Bentovim *et al.*, 1988a; Furniss, 1991; Dale *et al.*, 1986). At the other end are wider socio-cultural analyses of the structure and ideologies of society (MacLeod and Saraga, 1988b; Nelson, 1987; Russell, 1986; Finkelhor, 1988a).

In Britain, the analysis of child sexual abuse is dominated by one particular perspective, the 'dysfunctional family' theory. This sees family dynamics as a major cause of sexual abuse and identifies sexual abuse as something that occurs in 'deviant' families, where normal boundaries between parents and children have been breached (Dale *et al.*, 1986; Bentovim and Mrazek, 1981). Where the sexual relationship between the parents is unsatisfactory. it is argued, the father may turn his attention to his adolescent daughter, who may thereby gain status within the family and acquire the mother's role. Central to this perspective is the belief that mothers are collusive and culpable in the abuse. As a consequence, mothers are often accused of 'failure to protect'. Underlying this perspective is the assumption that 'scapegoating' occurs whereby all the family's problems become identified with one family member, leading to the abuse of that person. Proponents of this perspective claim that the scapegoating is necessary for the survival of the family and that responsibility for the abuse should involve all its members (Dale *et al.*, 1986).

Let us consider further the notion of breached boundaries. In sexual abuse cases, a situation exists where there is a child and an adult. The adult is often a parent, a figure of authority to the child, and one who has a responsibility to protect that child. Clearly the issue of boundaries is not what we need to be looking at here, but rather that of power dynamics. The suggestion that sexual abuse is part of a 'caring relationship' ignores the active initiation, and the use of force and coercion by men (Parton, 1990). The major problem with the dysfunctional family perspective is thus its failure to address the fact that sexual abuse is a gross misuse of power. By implicating all members of the family it avoids locating the blame at the feet of the (predominantly) male perpetrator, and fails to see sexual abuse as part of a continuum of male violence against women and children (Kelly, 1988).

The rise in the number of reported cases of sexual abuse means that increasing numbers of families are being drawn into the arena of child protection agencies. This places additional pressures on the women within these families who typically interact most frequently with social services departments. While the child is the primary client in a family where there is sexual abuse, children do not live in isolation. Their safe growth and development is dependent upon the quality of care provided by the adults in their lives. Social workers therefore have the difficult task of trying to maintain a balance between keeping the child with its own family, working with parents/carers, and keeping the needs of the child paramount.

To what extent are practitioners able to do this while at the same time successfully incorporating an analysis of gender and power dynamics? After the disclosure of abuse, mothers often have the difficult task of dealing with their own feelings of pain and anger, while also facing their child's rage at them for what their partners did (Russell, 1986). Practitioners have to enable women to address their feelings towards their partners and their child and at the same time encourage them to say to the child: 'He had no right to do this to you; I am glad you told me; it was not your fault.' Practitioners must recognise that the process from accepting to believing can take a long time. Some mothers may experience a range of feelings, such as anger, betrayal, guilt and denial, which may prevent them being able to validate the child's experience immediately. Not only have they been told that their child has been sexually abused, a daunting enough fact in itself, but they are then told that the abuser is not a stranger but a husband, partner: the child's father. The impact on a woman's sense of her own worth and status can be profound (Russell, 1986). Although some mothers have a lot of anger towards their partners, they may continue to have strong feelings of affection towards them. They can be torn between wanting to support their partners and wanting to protect their children (Russell, 1986). Some may feel anger towards their child for the break-up of their relationship.

The practitioners in my study felt that, rather than accusing the women of collusion, they had to be given time to work through this range of feelings and be allowed space to grieve, both for what had happened to their child and to themselves. To an extent, sexual abuse can place the mother and child in positions of mutual betrayal (Miller, 1990). The practitioners acknowledged that mothers faced with this situation need modes of social work intervention that recognise that the way they perceive themselves and their relationship with their partners, together with how they view the world, will change. Many of them become single parents virtually overnight. The full extent of the deep trauma that father–daughter incest causes mothers has been largely ignored (Russell, 1986).

A number of the practitioners in my study reported that they often felt that they were doing this work in total isolation. They were often conscious that their team managers were not sympathetic to their approach. While they felt they were making progress because a mother was for the first time expressing her feelings, they also had concerns about how this would be perceived at the next case conference where the focus of the discussion would be on the mother's parenting skills, and her ability to protect the child from further abuse.

The organisational setting

Practitioners incorporating feminist knowledge into their work have additional hurdles to overcome regarding the inherent conflicts in their role as statutory workers. The legal framework within which their practice is based and their system of accountability means they have a responsibility to explain to the mother the identified areas of concern, what is expected of her and, in return, what help and support she can expect to receive. This requires spelling out very clearly to a mother that practitioners may be required to enforce their legal role by removing her child, if they are not satisfied that she is doing all she can to protect her from further abuse. This is clearly a very difficult task. As a woman herself, the practitioner may feel empathy for, and the wish to be supportive of, her female client. A female practitioner, however, must be clear about the power differential that exists between herself and her female clients. Although as an individual she may see herself as relatively powerless within her agency, to the families she works with she is seen to wield its legal and organisational powers (Conn and Turner, 1990).

Practitioners in the study expressed their disquiet at modes of intervention that aimed to keep the family unit together at all costs, or to reconstitute the family without challenging the male abuse of power within it. The main criticisms were of traditional social work approaches rooted in 'treatment' methods that focus on women and encourage them to be good wives and mothers. So although it is overwhelmingly the men in the family who abuse, it is the women who are seen as inadequate and unable to cope. Such an approach blames the woman and obscures responsibility for the abuse. It reinforces the idea of the colluding mother and does nothing to challenge the male abuse of power within these families. More importantly, it serves to give a powerful message to the perpetrators that there is nothing implicitly wrong with their behaviour. As highlighted above, it is difficult to understand the pain and confusion of mothers who are treated as perpetrators, when they themselves have been victimised (Russell, 1986).

The practitioners in my study endeavoured to bring in modes of intervention that would start from women's strengths, and therefore actively acknowledge and utilise women's survival skills. Social work methods that are informed by a feminist perspective emphasise that the practitioner's role is to empower women, raise consciousness (of women in particular), place behaviour in its social context and encourage people to make choices and negotiate what they want out of family life (Masson and O'Byrne, 1990: 171). In attempting to allow women space to take some control of their lives, these practitioners actively rejected methods of working that reinforced assumptions that women are weak or masochistic. In order to encourage mothers to regain their confidence in themselves, they felt it was essential to allow them some control and choice. However, translating theory into practice brings its own problems for practitioners. The following example is a case in point:

A 6-year-old girl was abused by her father. The mother in this case was a strong capable woman who was working full time outside the home as well as carrying primary responsibility for the care of home and family. When the abuse came to light, she felt extremely guilty and felt that, had she been at home as a full-time mother, the abuse might not have occurred. This mother felt her only choice was to give up paid work and remain at home.

The practitioner in the above case observed that, despite her extreme anger at her husband, the mother nevertheless took some of the blame for the abuse of her daughter. She felt her approach should be to give the mother space to explore her feelings before she made any decisions about giving up her career. In so doing, this practitioner was accused by her male team manager of 'siding with the mother against the child and the father', and imposing her 'feminist' views on the mother. She was reminded by her manager that she should, at all times, remain neutral. The concept of neutrality relies on the notion of non-alliance with any family member. How then are practitioners to address gender inequality within the family if attempts to point out its existence bring accusations of 'taking sides'?

What this practitioner noted is the enormous psychological and social pressure on women to revert back to their perceived traditional role in society – that of wife and mother. It did not seem to matter that this was a successful, capable woman, with many strengths and therefore a good role model for her daughter. It was implied that her being at work full time probably did not help the matter. The implication was that she was 'absent' from her 'normal duties'. Views of the 'dysfunctional family' typically blame the weak or absent mother. The other more insidious assumption at work here is that '. . . daughters must be chaperoned in their own homes in order to be safe from abuse, and any mother who does not realise this and is not able to be an effective protector is at fault' (Russell, 1986: 384).

Several practitioners expressed their disquiet at being asked in case conferences about the state of the couple's sex life.

Often questions would be asked of the woman (not the man) to determine what she thought about their sexual relationship. These practitioners had refused to ask this as they felt that the underlying assumption was that, if the wife was satisfying her husband sexually, there would have been no need for him to look elsewhere for sexual release. The fact that the husband/ father is having 'marital' problems is frequently accepted in mitigation by the courts in cases of sexual abuse (Viinnikka, 1989). These practitioners were asked why they had not established this in their assessment interview. They replied that they felt such an approach would add to any guilt feelings that the mother may already have about being in some way responsible for the abuse of her child. It '. . . confirms the mother's image of herself as inadequate . . . and also attacks her capacity to care for and nuture her child' (Miller, 1990: 141). It also involves making women responsible for their partners' sexual feelings. In this way women are held accountable not just for their own behaviour and attitudes, but also for those of their husbands/partners (Brook and Davis, 1985). Moreover, the practice of ascertaining whether a couple's sex life is satisfactory helps to reinforce the common myth about the cause of sexual abuse: that if the wife is frigid and rejects her husband's advances, this can lead him into abuse (Nelson, 1987). As Parton (1990) argues, if we accept this view then we are accepting the notion that it is a man's right to have sexual services on demand.

Problems and dilemmas of inter-agency work

The management of child sexual abuse cases dictates that inter-agency liaison is essential. This means that all agencies involved with a family have to work and make decisions together. A number of child abuse enquiries (Beckford in 1985, Henry in 1984, and Cleveland in 1987) have highlighted the inadequacy of the individual responses of caring agencies. As a result, the Department of Health document *Working*

Together Under the Children Act, 1989 (HMSO, 1991b) spelled out the conditions under which all agencies with responsibilities in the child protection process (social services, health services, police, schools, probation and the NSPCC), together with other personnel who can offer expert advice (for example, psychiatrists, psychologists and lawyers) are required to work collaboratively for the protection of children. The child protection conference, which is central to child protection procedures, brings together the family and the professionals concerned. This is the key forum for sharing information and concerns, analysing risk, and making recommendations for action. It can be crucial in influencing the outcome of a case.

The practitioners in my study felt that, on the whole, the inter-agency framework did not facilitate an environment where it was safe to discuss gender and oppression. They perceived the inter-agency set-up as hierarchical, with the social work practitioner (who often tends to be the one working most closely with the family) typically having the lowest status. It is within this framework that practitioners have to outline their assessment of the problem, and make their recommendations about what work should be done with a family. Practitioners felt that at times other professionals so influence the outcome that it is difficult for them to bring in a perspective that is informed by feminist knowledge.

The following extract from one practitioner's experience exemplifies this:

A 6-year-old girl made allegations that she had been sexually abused by the headmaster of her school. Despite several attempts by her mother to bring this to the attention of agencies, no one would take her seriously. Finally, out of desperation, the mother wrote to several agencies – the Education Department, the Director of Social Services, local councillors, etc. In the ensuing furore, several case conferences were convened. However, the attention seemed to focus on the mother in a very negative way. She was labelled as 'hysterical', 'neurotic' and 'going around accusing men of abusing her child'. The police officer at the case conference suggested that, as a single mother, she may have had different boyfriends, and one of them may have abused the child.

At the third case conference, the psychiatrist present informed the meeting that it was highly probable that the child had been abused, because her story was consistent with the person and the setting where the alleged abuse took place. The practitioner felt that it was only after the psychiatrist made his claims that the other professionals reluctantly came round to accepting the idea that the child had indeed been abused. The main concern seemed to be not that the child had been abused, but that the 'alleged' abuser was a headmaster, and a member of the inter-agency network. Although the professionals could not call on their theories of the dysfunctional family to explain the abuse, they nevertheless focused on mother-blaming tactics. Her suggestions for working in ways with the mother that did not blame or scapegoat her invoked the criticism that she was making value judgements. It was implied by the other professionals that she was inexperienced, and therefore 'allowing her emotions to get the better of her'.

What emerges from the above example is the way in which other professionals may accuse practitioners of making value judgements, in order to dismiss their ideas. It is interesting to note that although the police officer made claims about the mother, he was not accused of letting his emotions get the better of him. We are led to believe that his assertions were not value-laden, but professional judgements. It would seem that accusations of value judgement are more likely to be made about views that appear to challenge prevailing norms. A view that supports the status quo is seen as neutral. Protests from practitioners who come up against this may occasion further accusations of 'letting their personal feelings get in the way of their professional duties'.

On this evidence it seems that attempts to challenge gender oppression are met with a very similar response to that given to mothers of abused children. They are either marginalised, scapegoated, or left doubting their abilities. It appears that a commitment to address gender inequalities and show sensitivity to the needs of mothers is in contradiction to working in the best interest of the child. Yet it could be argued that working with mothers in ways that do not blame or scapegoat them is also in the best interest of the child. The mother who receives a sympathetic response is more likely to be able to offer her abused child sensitive care.

The dimension of race and gender

The complexities of race and gender can exacerbate the problems for practitioners and serve to mask the realities of black girls' and women's experience in the family. The following account provides an example of this. A white practitioner describes her attempts to work in a positive, non-sexist way with a British-born Bengali young woman:

> This 15-year-old young woman had been sexually abused by an uncle. As a result, she had started to truant from school and developed other behavioural problems with which her parents had difficulties coping. Her parents felt the solution was to send her to Bangladesh - something this young woman did not want. The practitioner outlined the available options, and allowed her space to explore them. She was criticised by her team manager – a white female – who felt that the family could accuse the Department of being racist by imposing western feminist ideas on the young woman. The practitioner in turn felt that her manager was making stereotypical assumptions about Asian families.

In offering assistance to people of a different race and social class, it is essential to understand their viewpoints especially their culture and values about family life. While this practitioner's manager was keen to address herself to good social work practice with black families, she was ignoring the wishes of the young woman. Ascertaining the views of the child is strongly stressed in the 1989 Children Act. However, it seemed to this practitioner that the message she was being given by her manager was that, in this case, the wishes and feelings of the child did not matter, because they could result in accusations of racism. The practitioner recognised the practice dilemmas: she must give due consideration to the wishes and feelings of the child, while at the same time respecting the rights of the parents and seeing the welfare of the black child in the context of his/her race, religion and language. Problematically, she was not able to discuss the complexities of this situation and the conflict it presented for her.

This example demonstrates the problem of insufficient cultural knowledge, which results in an inability to distinguish between understanding and respecting other cultures and holding stereotypical notions about those cultures. What is manifest in this case is the way a nervousness around race can act to cloud the issues around gender oppression in black families. A reluctance to take account of gender inequalities in black families can mean that black girls are left in abusive situations, or decisions are made that are not in their best interests. The outcome is that, by desperately trying to work in an anti-racist way, some practitioners can end up acting unintentionally in both racist and sexist ways.

In contrast, the following experience of a black practitioner challenging gender oppression raises different issues:

A black female practitioner was involved with a white family who were foster carers, and had two children of their own – young men aged 15 and 17. They had three children placed with them: a brother and sister aged seven and six and another child, a boy age five. The brother and sister made serious allegations of sexual abuse by the foster father and son aged 17. While the child abuse investigation was going on, in accordance with this authority's policy either all children placed with the family should have been removed, or the father and son should have been asked to leave the family home. It was suggested, however, that only the brother and sister making the allegations should be removed.The other child should remain on the understanding that he should not be left alone with the father and the older son. The practitioner disagreed with this on the basis that it left the responsibility with the foster mother to see that her husband and son were not left alone with the child. This, she felt, placed the mother in an untenable position. It seemed to her that the mother was being asked to take responsibility for the behaviour of both her husband and son. She was overruled by her white male manager who went ahead and made the decision, thus undermining her.The practitioner felt this involved two negative issues. First-ly, based on her observations of the way her manager interacts with her colleagues, she felt he would have acted differently had it been one of her white colleagues – regardless of their gender. She felt that she was accorded less respect than them. More impor-tantly, she felt this significantly altered her relationship with the family. Being aware of the way her manager undermined her, the family – and in particular the foster father – now seemed reluctant to respect her professional judgement. She therefore had to work harder to build up a rapport again.

We cannot say for certain that this practitioner's manager would have acted in the same way if the race and gender of the practitioner had been different. Nevertheless, what is high-lighted by the above example is the way not only the power dynamics between managers and basic grade workers can influence outcomes, but how the influence of racism adds another very different dimension. While this practitioner was attempting to challenge one form of gender oppression, another form of gender oppression, interlinked with the dynamics of racism, was acting against her.

What we see from the above examples is how significant social divisions may militate against a female practitioner being able to identify with her female client solely on the basis that they share the same gender identity. Perceptive practi-tioners must be able to understand not only the power differentials that exist between them and their female clients, but also the relations of power inherent in gender, class, disability, sexual orientation and race. Practitioners should also be aware of the diversity of ethnic experiences that are a result of factors like religion and caste (Anthias and Yuval-Davis, 1992). This awareness should inform understanding of the specific ways in which different groups of women experience the abuse of their children, and the differential treatment they receive from statutory agencies. Without this analysis, practitioners will not understand how their female clients' subjective experience interacts with wider social and political structures. More importantly, without this broader understanding there are far-reaching implications for a feminist social work practice that seeks to engage all women.

Practitioners' support networks

In order to help practitioners establish a clear position in their work with families, it is important that they receive regular competent supervision from their own professional support system (Conn and Turner, 1990). Practitioners should be able to use supervision to look at their work and to improve their practice. Managers have a duty to be available to offer support, guidance and advice to practitioners. They also have a duty to help practitioners to be clear about the reasons for casework decisions (BASW, 1988). In practice, the unequal distribution of power between practitioner and supervisor, both in terms of hierarchical position and issues around gender and race, militates against this happening. In general, the nature of the relationship between the supervisor and practitioner does not provide a good framework for practitioners to discuss subjects that may be painful or difficult. For practitioners incorporating feminist ideas into their work, this raises other problems. The practitioners in my study claimed that when they sought to incorporate feminist theory, they were not given adequate opportunity for reflective supervision. They felt that their managers were either unaware of or felt threatened by (or, in some instances, were openly hostile to) modes of intervention that had at their core an understanding of how gender and power dynamics operate.

Practitioners generally felt that they were not encouraged to discuss the impact of working with child sexual abuse. It appeared that the acknowledgement that such work made them feel angry, confused or powerless was seen as a sign of weakness, or not coping (see also Chapter 7 in this volume). If practitioners are nervous about applying feminist knowledge to their practice in the first place, this makes it even more difficult for them to explore their feelings with their managers. The end result is that they are encouraged to privatise the problems associated with the work, which increases their sense of powerlessness. Additionally, for those practitioners who are inexperienced in the area of child sexual abuse work, these difficulties add to their perception of the problems as their own personal failure. Thus, in the process of trying to appear professional and objective, the practitioner may internalise some of the value conflicts inherent in the notion of a social work practice that is supposedly value-free and neutral.

One of the best strategies for child sexual abuse work is co-working (Glaser and Frosh, 1988). This enables one practitioner to work with the abused child, while another works with the mother. This can help to keep a sharper focus on the specific issues that arise for the mother without losing sight of the paramountcy of the child's interests. From the practitioners' point of view, two workers can help to reduce the level of stress involved in carrying the statutory responsibility for a case. It also allows co-workers the opportunity to off-load to each other which can help allieviate anxieties. However, practitioners felt that suggestions for co-working are still not fully accepted in a profession that reinforces the notion of individual responsibility. Lack of available resources are often given as the reason why co-working is not encouraged. Although lack of resources is clearly a major factor, this may not be the only reason. Practitioners felt that this argument was often based on the anxieties of some practitioners and managers about opening up their practice to greater scrutiny. It seems that practitioners were left to develop their own support networks and coping strategies. These included networking with practitioners who shared similar perspectives, together with keeping up to date with relevant feminist and other progressive writings. Practitioners felt that these measures helped to sustain their motivation and reduce feelings of isolation.

Conclusions: the implications of integrating feminist theory with practice

In summary, it seems that a common concern for practitioners working within an anti-oppressive framework is the fear that they will be accused of letting their personal views interfere with their professional duties. This supports the broadly held view in social work that professionalism is about being objective and neutral. Starting from this position, however, fails to acknowledge that social work is neither neutral nor value-free, and is not carried out in a vacuum (Shardlow, 1989). It is a political activity that is informed by broader social and ideological beliefs about gender, class, race and sexual orientation. Methods of intervention therefore must be steeped in an understanding of how the social construction of gender relations in the family interrelates with other significant social divisions such as race and class. Practitioners must understand that these play a central role in shaping the way both children and their mothers experience the impact of sexual abuse on their lives. Not to acknowledge this may be to promote a view that supports the status quo and ultimately gives tacit support to those who abuse children.

Although the research I have undertaken suggests that it is a difficult struggle for practitioners, it is heartening to discover that, despite the obstacles facing them within their agency structures, many have a strong commitment to challenge gender oppression in social work practice. The one factor motivating them is the belief that anti-oppressive practice is at the core of good social work practice. For them, not challenging discriminatory attitudes and practice would mean that, in the words of one practitioner: 'the majority of social services clients, women and children, would get a very poor service'. It is hoped that this chapter will help practitioners identify a number of important issues and challenges posed in the attempt to work from an anti-oppressive stance. In addition, it may serve to facilitate an understanding of some of the value conflicts inherent in translating feminist theory into practice in the area of child sexual abuse.

Note

1. This is based on a small-scale study conducted with professionally qualified social work practitioners working in an inner-city local authority setting. The non-random sample comprised four white females, three Asian females, two Afro-Caribbean females and one white male. This breakdown broadly reflected the social composition of the social workers employed by the authority.

6

Prostitution and the State: Towards a Feminist Practice

Maggie O'Neill

> Prostitution will remain a crime in this country, and in other.
> countries which criminalise it, so long as there is no identifiable
> voting bloc that clamours for change in the law. . . Prostitutes get
> scapegoated for AIDS and few people cry out. Prostitutes are
> murdered and the police tell no-one until ten or more have been
> killed by one person. And even then there is little outcry in the
> square world. . .
>   None of this will change, it seems to me, until prostitutes speak
> out in all their varied voices. . . . Almost all of us worked in the
> industry at some time in our lives; a few of us have never literally
> done sexual work, although our lives were filled with allusions to
> it. All of us are united in wanting an end to the pain in women's
> lives, an end to abuse, an end to violence (Delacoste and
> Alexander, 1988: 16–18).

Introduction

As a feminist, my approach is to place women's voices at the
very heart of my research. For me, 'doing' feminist research
involves relating women's experiences to the development of
feminist theory and to the generation of practice aimed at
policy change. Creating a space for women's voices is central
to the process of understanding that must accompany social
change, and this entails working *with* women as well as *for*
them and engaging in the politics of empowerment (O'Neill,
1992a).

My work in the East Midlands began in 1990 with a pilot study to explore current responses to prostitution and to suggest multi-agency initiatives to deal with the 'problem'.[1] Out of this initial study grew a very active multi-agency forum on prostitution regularly attended by women working as prostitutes. Three further projects also emerged: an examination of the relationship between prostitution and feminism(s), an action-research project exploring routes into prostitution from local authority care and a small project funded by the European Social Fund that examined exit possibilities related to counselling, guidance, education and training for women working as prostitutes.

In this chapter I argue the need for the whores' movement and the feminist movement to come together to discuss the central issues involved in women working as prostitutes,[2] and to join forces in support of women working in the sex industry and dealing with interrelated inequalities in the spheres of violence, sexuality, work and power. In order to address sexual and social inequalities in these linked spheres, they must be explored in the wider context of the role and power of the 'masculinist' state (Walby, 1990)[3] and against the global socio-economic backdrop to female prostitution. Feminists and whores need to work together to explore these related issues and to identify future strategies for challenging and resisting sexual and social inequalities and for the development of women-centred alternatives. This means encouraging effective resistance to women's poverty[4] and to the commodification and 'exchange value' of the female body.[5] Attempting to change state policy in line with feminist objectives entails a thorough analysis and critique of state policy, with a view to revealing its masculinist nature and operation. It also involves the struggle to 'feminise' the process of central decision-making by creating the intellectual and practical space for women's voices to be heard, and by the greater representation of women at all levels of the state and state-related agencies, particularly at managerial and decision-making levels.

The theoretical and personal foundations for this work are located in my commitment to what can be termed 'participatory action research' (O'Neill, 1992b). Taking an ethnographic approach and immersing myself in the 'lived experience' of prostitute women led to our working together – alongside representatives from statutory and voluntary agencies – to try and effect some change in local policies relating to the general disempowerment of street prostitutes and the violence they experience. By working with POW! (Prostitute Outreach Workers) and members of the multi-agency forum on prostitution, we were able to address the anomalies experienced by women as a result of what Pheterson (1986) has called the 'whore stigma'. We were also able to identify and challenge the attitudes that serve to reinforce acceptable levels of violence against women prostitutes.

This chapter aims to outline the specifically feminist research I have conducted in the East Midlands since 1990 and highlight the centrality of violence in the lived experience of prostitute women. It also aims to locate this work in a critique of the 'masculinist state' and in the wider debate about the legalisation or decriminalisation of prostitution.

'Doing' feminist research

There are three interrelated dimensions to my work: my own critical theoretical perspective on the working of the state and state power; the creation of the intellectual and practical space for the voices and experiences of women involved in doing sex work and finally, the engagement in practical work to support and empower women sex workers and to challenge and resist sexual and social inequalities. Taken together, these three dimensions of theory, experience and practice are woven into a central focus of concern, which is about 'being' a feminist researcher and 'doing' feminist research that has practical implications and possibilities for the women involved as 'subjects' of that research. While I do not propose here to provide solutions to the methodological and epistemological problems inherent in doing feminist research, I can at the very least share my experiences, concerns and attempts to resolve some of the dilemmas involved. Stanley (1990) discusses the need for feminist knowledge to be defined not simply as 'knowledge what' but as 'knowledge for': as knowledge that underpins and informs feminist practice. It is in this spirit of 'feminist praxis' that my own endeavours are grounded.

During the course of my work the relationship between my theoretical way of seeing and my understanding of sex workers' lived relations has been reflexive. Talking with the women involved raised issues and problems for my theory. Indeed, from this reflexive relationship came the urgent need to engage in a feminist practice that was policy-oriented and that addressed some of the specific problems and issues raised by the women. This practice involved engaging in multi-agency work (a grouping of sex workers and committed representatives from statutory and non-statutory agencies) to address three central issues: routes into prostitution; routes out of prostitution; and support for women who want to work as sex workers, or for whom there is no immediate possibility of exit.

Responses to prostitution in the East Midlands: a woman-centred, multi-agency approach

I felt it was important that this study looked at the factors underlying street prostitution in the East Midlands and examined the wider socio-political issues involved in women's entry into prostitution. Further, I considered it significant that the research should examine the interplay between the various statutory and voluntary agencies concerned with prostitution and women who work the beat. The first stage of the project thus involved interviewing all the central agencies, as well as talking with the prostitute women, to identify the parameters of the problem. Discussions with the women involved an ethnographic research approach that avoided the use of structured interviews, clipboards or dictaphones. Initially the women were wary and suspicious of my project and what I was going to do with the information. Ethically, I felt it was important to let the women know exactly what I was doing and why I wanted to talk to them. I found that by not pushing them into conversation, by simply taking time to 'get to know' them, I experienced friendliness and a willingness to talk and share conversation.

The second stage involved outlining areas of commonality and difference between the agencies and the women, with a view to developing multi-agency initiatives. The third stage was the organisation of a half-day seminar inviting all the agencies whose representatives I had interviewed. This served the threefold purpose of feeding back information to the various agencies, facilitating discussion of the proposals in multi-agency discussion groups, and enabling the agencies to own and cooperate with the proposals that emerged.

The main areas of commonality between the agencies and the prostitute women included: concern for the health, welfare and safety of sex workers, and acknowledgement that violence is a central aspect of sex workers' lives; concern for the often vulnerable young women entering prostitution and the need to know more about routes into prostitution, as well as possible options for those wishing to exit prostitution.The statutory agencies were trusted less by the women than the voluntary agencies. The latter were seen as less controlling, as more 'on their side'. The issue of confidentiality was central here, with those agencies that provided a confidential service being trusted and used by the women.

Outcomes

It was felt by the agencies represented in the study that the main areas of common concern focused upon the practicalities of the women's daily lives. I suggested that statutory and voluntary bodies could work together (through a multi-agency forum) to develop an integrative strategy to educate people, to facilitate the more effective use of health services, and to improve the knowledge and use of safe-sex practices – as well as to address the endemic nature of violence against the women and the need for advice and counselling services. Furthermore, I put forward the proposal that key agencies could provide a more closely organised network of services to address material, economic and social/emotional needs, as well as encouraging self-help and peer-group empowerment. Services could be coordinated in the short term through a street-level centre provided by, and for, sex workers and, in the longer term, by addressing policy change at local, regional and national levels. The report was well received by the agencies involved and the 'East Midlands Forum into Prostitution' was established as a result. Representatives from the major agencies gave their commitment to the need for more research and action on the welfare, health, safety and legal concerns raised within the Forum. In particular they agreed to develop more knowledge on the routes into and out of sex work and to encourage better support networks with, and for, women engaged in prostitution.

Violence as a central aspect of sex workers' lives

The endemic fact of male violence against women in our society – which is marked by an often inappropriate response on the part of the state – is a central aspect of the lived relations of all women, but perhaps more particularly prostitute women (Hoigard and Finstad, 1992; O'Neill, 1991b, 1992a; Delacoste and Alexander, 1988; Jaget, 1980). The sex workers I talked to in my initial pilot study were mostly aged between eighteen and twenty-four. All the women I spoke with had entered prostitution for financial reasons, and all had been in local authority care or had problematic family backgrounds. All the women except one had entered prostitution by association – that is to say, all but one knew someone else who was working the streets or engaged in sex work. All had experienced violence from clients. One woman had recently been severely beaten and had her throat cut by a client. She is alive and recovering. This incident was not reported in the local press. Other incidents that women talked about include rapes and beatings. Some women had experienced violence from partners, although I did not feel at this early stage in the development of relationships of trust that I could ask the women about their domestic partners or the men who acted as pimps.

The East Midlands' police were concerned about gathering enough data on the violent men involved with sex workers to get a successful prosecution without the evidence of the women, for the women are notorious in their withdrawal of evidence. Women working as prostitutes are often loath to report rapes, assaults and incidences of violence and harassment to statutory agencies. The reason they give is quite clear: they are worried that they will not be taken seriously and that they will be treated as 'deserving victims'. Women have told me of horrifying assaults that have not been taken seriously by agencies such as police and residential-care staff. 'What do you expect if you are on the game?' is a common response. Some women are loath to contact Women's Aid refuges as staff insist that they do not work while they are in residence.

Our multi-agency forum has acted as an information pool and a forum where representatives from various agencies can begin to improve upon services offered to working women, particularly in the light of violence against women. Probation services offer women's groups, assertiveness training and much-needed information about the criminal injuries compensation scheme, and can refer women on to prostitute support groups such as POW! (Prostitute Outreach Workers). The police have changed their policies in that there is no longer a requirement that victims of assault be present in court to give evidence against their assailant. The vice squad have also purchased more safety alarms wired up to the central police station to protect women at risk of violence, and possibly death, from known assailants. POW! offers safe houses to women, support, counselling and guidance to 'victims' of violence, as well as peer-empowerment and education. One part of POW!'s service is to refer women on to representatives in the relevant agencies at both statutory and voluntary level. Social services, particularly residential care and staff concerned with young people moving from residential care into local communities, are finding the work of POW! and the Forum helpful in supporting both young women involved in prostitution and those trying to leave.

In my conversations with women involved in street sex work, and from the evidence in the available literature, street sex workers appear to have a rather clinical, matter-of-fact, way of talking about the violence they experience. As an everyday occurrence, it is viewed by the women as part of the job. They learn to cope and handle situations of potential violence. Women have talked to me of 'gentling' potentially violent clients – some have expressed it as 'getting inside their heads' – in order to deal with them and protect themselves. Others have 'allowed' rape and indecent assaults to happen in order to save themselves from greater harm. Hoigard and Finstad (1992: 62) suggest that this is a survival strategy – the abnormal becoming normal – in an attempt to deny the significance of what is happening. In Hoigard and Finstad's study it was the clients who were responsible for most of the violence against prostitutes. The authors document explosions of rage and also more insidious planned attacks upon female prostitutes. They also illuminate the informal support networks operating between groups of women; for example, the way the women 'look out' for each other and develop strategies to diffuse potentially violent situations.

Hoigard and Finstad describe the road to prostitution as a breakdown in the women's respect for themselves (p. 19). In my experience, this is not always the case. Entry into prostitution, for some women, is marked by their taking control of their lives and resisting poverty for themselves and their children. This could be described as rational-choice action. Hoigard and Finstad also describe prostitution as violence against women (p. 114), and indeed this is often the case. As a feminist I feel that we need fundamentally to address the sexual and social relations in which prostitution and violence take place. We need to explore the wider social and economic contexts of women's involvement in sex work, the social construction of sexual inequalities and the organisation of desire in our society. Although there is not space to explore these issues here, it is important to acknowledge that while prostitution can be viewed as violence against women, there is something much more complex going on between clients and prostitutes in the wider context of social attitudes towards the body, sexuality and sexual practices.

Multi-agency, women-centred working groups based around the twin concepts of empowerment and resistance, and centrally involving sex workers, are one way of addressing the needs and problems experienced by prostitute women and the agencies with whom they have contact. With the women's involvement, multi-agency initiatives informed by wider social, legal and economic processes can move forward in a more informed way, challenging, resisting – and, hopefully, changing – specific policies and, in part, wider sexual and social inequalities.

Recognising that sex workers have minimal citizenship rights, this is something we must all address. In the campaign for women's rights it is important to recognise that prostitutes are women first, and that there should be no divisions in the support for women's rights. The whore's movement and the feminist movement need to join forces to address the contradictions and sexual and social inequalities in all women's lives within the interrelated spheres of work, sexuality, power and violence. Addressing these inequalities through a critique of the 'masculinist state' is vital to feminist theory and practice.

The role and power of the 'masculinist' state

It is important to contextualise the multi-agency work ongoing in the East Midlands and the violence experienced by women prostitutes within an understanding of the wider role and power of the masculinist state. In addressing this issue I am concerned with the violence experienced by all women, in both public and private spheres, at the level of lived experience and at the level of the state. The operation of the legal system, court policy and the policing of street sex workers all increase the risk of violence, disease and emotional stress to women for whom, out of economic or emotional need, prostitution is work. The state indirectly sanctions unequal power relations between men and women by the lack of effective action taken against violence against all women, but more particularly against those women who are seen as less worthy, as deviant or as wayward women.

Observation of the ways in which prostitute women are policed and treated by the criminal justice system can provide evidence of the workings of one aspect of the masculinist state. The way women are treated in court is alienating and intimidating. They are rarely addressed personally, mostly they are discussed in the third person as 'offenders'. The level of fines given to women in the East Midlands has increased since 1989, in response to the complaints of residents living in the vice area who demanded action by the police and legal system. At the same time, the police engaged in 'high profile policing' of the vice area both to deter women from working (the supply) and to deter kerb crawlers (the demand).

In the East Midlands the women are constantly arrested, pimps are also targeted, as are kerb crawlers and men who solicit the favours of a 'common prostitute'. Women are fined heavily and often cannot make contact with sufficient clients to pay off their fines and make a living. In addition, they may also have to pay a pimp or support their partner. As a result, women often move away to work in unfamiliar towns and cities, exposing themselves to greater risks. They may 'take' clients without the necessary 'sussing-out' time. They may not be familiar with the informal networks that operate between women, and may be at risk from violence and even death.

The state as an 'institutional form of political power'

Offe (1984) describes the state as the 'institutional form of political power' underpinned in capitalist societies by the myth of 'democratic and representative government'. The 'material content' of capitalist state power (its policies and practice) is conditioned by the 'continued requirements of the accumulation process'. Walby (1990) maintains that the state reinforces the subordination and oppression of women through the workings of the legal system and via social policy. The state, she claims, is both 'masculinist' and the outcome of 'competing political pressures'. Furthermore, despite some changes in gender relations in the last 150 years, Walby claims that the state is still patriarchal, capitalist and racist (1990: 171). As an institutional form of political power, the state is predisposed to favour the interests of capital over and above the interests of women experiencing economic hardship and violence within and outside the sphere of prostitution. Taken together, Offe's and Walby's accounts of the nature and operation of state power provide us with a useful analytical framework for developing a critique of the relationship between the state and prostitution in Britain and North America.

A central implication of New Right social and economic policies throughout the 1980s and into the 1990s has been the growth in the 'feminisation' of poverty (Matthews, 1986; Glendinning, 1987; Carlen, 1988; O'Neill, 1992a, b), the rise in unemployment, the restructuring of the economy and the development of a new underclass (Lash, 1992). What do these tendencies mean for the sex industry and women working as prostitutes? First, the institutional power of the state welcomes the revenue that is brought in by the sex industry.

A masculinist state will not be overly concerned that women are subjected to violence, abuse, degradation and pain in the process of capital accumulation from the sex industry. Second, these tendencies have effectively increased the number of people suffering poverty, homelessness, crime and emotional stress. As a result, more and more women and young girls are turning to prostitution out of economic need. Some young women, moving into prostitution from local authority care, also turn to prostitution through emotional neediness. These young women are often vulnerable, lonely and lacking in a sense of self-worth.

In order to develop resistance and empowerment, feminism and the whores' movement need to acknowledge and work with these central issues. For some women prostitution is work; for others it is an escape from violence, abuse and disempowering social backgrounds towards 'greater economic autonomy' and 'personal freedom'.[6] Lastly, we must acknowledge that the central contradictions in these sex workers' lived relations are not too different from the central contradictions in all women's lives, as documented by Ramazanoglu (1989).

Prostitution, the state and the decriminalisation or legalisation debate

Prostitution in Britain is not illegal; the laws that criminalise prostitution have been abolished. However, the 'nuisance value' of soliciting in a public place is a crime. In Britain, a woman can work as a prostitute as long as she does not solicit publicly, advertise the sale of sex, live with another woman (they could be prosecuted for operating a brothel) or live with a man (he could be prosecuted for living off immoral earnings). Furthermore, she is often stigmatised and castigated by feminists and non-feminists alike. She operates through what Pheterson (1986) has called the 'whore stigma'. Her crime is a crime against morality; she is not fully 'woman', she is 'other'. Many women working in the sex industry lead double lives. They operate under false names to protect their work identity, their children and relatives from knowing about their work and in order to negotiate the cautioning system.[7] In Britain, the unintended effects of the operation of the legal system in controlling and policing street prostitution brings violence, fear of arrest and prosecution with attendant fines. In the East Midlands, as elsewhere, some fines are so high that women cannot pay them, and they are subsequently imprisoned for the offence of fine default. Furthermore, to pay their fines women must continue to work within prostitution. There is no national standard for fining women for the offence of soliciting (Golding, 1992) and hefty fines are frequently imposed.

Prostitution *per se* is not a crime, but it is a crime to solicit publicly, and it is perceived as a crime against morality. Women are subject to abuse and violence from clients, pimps and domestic partners. Furthermore, they can be imprisoned for non-payment of fines, and their children can be accommodated into care while they are serving a prison sentence or if they are not perceived as 'good enough' mothers. Women who are 'known prostitutes' have a harder time than 'normal' women in trying to get the police to take assault from male partners seriously (Hoigard and Finstad, 1992). Women working in the sex industry are thus dealt a double injustice: they are criminalised for their whore status, and at one and the same time they are criminalised for being poor and for resisting poverty.

For Delacoste and Alexander (1988), strategies including decriminalising prostitution and regulating pimping and procuring offer the best chance for women working in the sex industry to gain control of their work (p. 210). The International Collective for Prostitutes' Rights argues that women have the right to work as prostitutes and are entitled to the same human rights and civil liberties as other workers. The First European Whores' Congress which took place in Frankfurt am Main in October 1991, voted upon a resolution to be included in the European Community's Charter of the social rights of the employee. This stated that 'prostitution is a reality in society. It is a service that every person can offer or seek'. This leads us to consider whether legalisation or decriminalisation operationalised by the state are the answers to the problems faced by women working in street prostitution.

Legalisation

The example set by European countries such as Denmark, Holland, Germany and some parts of the USA shows us categorically that regulating prostitution, setting up zones of tolerance or municipal/state brothels is not the answer. Delacoste and Alexander tell us:

> The brothels in Nevada, for example, are licensed and regulated by the government, and the women who work in them are registered as prostitutes with the sheriff. . . . The women generally work fourteen hour shifts, on three week (seven days a week) tours of duty, during which they may see ten or fifteen customers a day, or more. They have little or no right to refuse a customer (although the management tries to keep out potentially dangerous customers), and they have not been allowed to protect themselves from sexually transmitted diseases by using condoms. . . . Because of the gruelling aspects of the long work shifts, many of the women use drugs (to help them stay awake and alert or to help them sleep) supplied by the same doctor who performs regular health checks (1988: 210).

In the Federal Republic of Germany (FRG) prostitution is also regulated and takes place in a variety of locations including brothels, eros centres, streets, clubs and bars and via escort services. Women working as prostitutes must pay income tax even though under German law to work as a prostitute affords no rights in law – as prostitution is considered an offence against morality. The names and personal data of prostitutes are registered by the police and health authorities. Prostitutes *must* attend for health checks every one to four weeks. Pimping is punished, as is the 'support' of prostitution. So a brothel keeper or club owner offering good working conditions could be prosecuted and imprisoned (Droessler, 1991: 19). For the last ten years prostitute organisations have been campaigning to change the laws and have been representing the human and political rights of sex workers. HYDRA in Berlin and HWG in Frankfurt are but two organisations operating in the FRG calling for the de-criminalisation of the law.

Thus legalisation, or state control of prostitution, does not address the key issues that the whores' movement sees as central to the civil liberties and human rights of women engaged in sex work. Legalisation ensures that the state acts as pimp, sanctioning prostitution at the same time as criminalising those women engaged in sex work outside of state control. Prostitution and the wider sex industry bring in huge revenues. Women enter, and are encouraged to remain in, prostitution out of economic need through the state sanctioning 'controlled' and 'regulated' prostitution. On the one hand, women are criminalised for being whores, but on the other hand state action enables women to use prostitution to earn a living. Through the legalisation of prostitution in certain areas, buildings or zones of tolerance, the state sanctions women's sale of their bodies on the open market to men who have the spending power to exchange money for the use of these bodies. I maintain that the relationship between use value and exchange value is a central moral problem for feminism and one that we need to address in our dialogue with the whores' movement.

Decriminalisation

Regional, national and international prostitute organisations in Britain and the USA support the 'World Charter for Prostitutes Rights' in making the following demands: the decriminalisation of all aspects of adult prostitution; the enforcement of criminal laws against fraud, coercion, child abuse, rape and racism everywhere; the need to guarantee prostitutes human rights and civil liberties; the freedom for prostitutes to choose their place of work and residence; the right of prostitutes to organise collectively; the right to health education; an end to mandatory health checks unless *all adults* are given mandatory checks; the establishment of exit routes for prostitutes via safe houses and retraining programmes that should be publicly funded; the payment by prostitutes of regular taxes and their entitlement to receive the same social welfare benefits as the rest of the population; the funding of educational programmes that help the public to understand and not to stigmatise prostitutes; the protection of financial autonomy, occupational choice and sexual self-determination and the creation of a movement to foster all women's rights. Given these demands, there is clearly ground for feminists and the whores' movement to form alliances, and develop common goals and strategies for working together to challenge sexual and social inequalities.Those who advocate decriminalisation call for all laws around prostitution to be dropped. This approach demands that women be allowed to operate as prostitutes how, when and where they like. Prostitution should be accepted legally and morally as a profession, as work. The central problem with this approach, as with that of legalisation, is that the use value of women's bodies is then enshrined in law, via state policy.

State sanction of prostitution as a legal profession legitimates the use value of women's bodies and the exchange value inherent in the servicing of men's bodies for money. Matthews (1986) points out that the decriminalisation or state regulation of prostitution (non-intervention) ensures revenue in the form of taxes, and a decrease in the cost of policing. Matthews goes on to outline the central problem inherent in decriminalising prostitution. State non-intervention underpins a 'commitment to nominalism'; that is to say, the problem is seen in terms of individual choice or motivation, *not* economic and political social relations:

Decriminalization minimizes the important role of protective legislation which, however paternalistic, recognizes the real vulnerability of certain groups of women. There is nothing very radical in turning a blind eye to the wide range of asymmetrical power relations within society between classes, sexes and races (Matthews, 1986: 199).

For Matthews, decriminalisation reinforces non-interventionist arguments founded upon nominalism 'rather than offering a critical alternative' (p. 198).

It seems to me that decriminalising and/or legalising prostitution lets the state 'off the hook' in addressing and fundamentally dealing with the feminisation of poverty and the double standards that are indicative of sexual and social relations in our society. State regulation or decriminalisation of prostitution simply reinforces the masculinist basis of state power, the role of the state as pimp and the growing individualism that has marked state activity in Britain and North America in the post-war period.

The 'regulationist' strategies that European and some North American states have pursued are based upon individual choice at the expense of acknowledging wider social relations. Strategies based upon individual choice serve to deflect attention from capitalist sexual, social and economic relations, the activities of a masculinist state, and the possible outcomes in the lived relations of female prostitutes' lives.

What, then, is the answer? I do not propose to offer a ready solution here. However, there are two alternative strategies that could be considered. First, Matthews (1986) suggests radical regulationism as an alternative. Radical regulationism operates within the framework of the legal system and the current operation of state activity and state power. This perspective views 'prostitution as a social and historical and, therefore, transformable product, rather than a "natural" or trans-historical entity' (p. 204). Acknowledging the limitations of existing legislation, radical regulationism is committed to a general deterrence, the reduction of harassment and disturbance, protection from coercion and exploitation and the reduction of commercialisation. Radical regulationism presents rational and achievable changes in the law to protect women from coercion, exploitation and criminalisation. It does this while maintaining a distance from the position of accepting prostitution as suitable work and within a framework that acknowledges the objectives of feminism. In this sense, radical regulationism achieves feminist as well as socialist objectives although not, I would argue, from a woman-centred perspective.

In creating an alternative strategy that necessarily operates within the current framework of the legal system, Matthews's analysis fails to address the central problem of the power and position of the masculinist state. Nor does it challenge the state's role in the relationship between prostitution and poverty, or in sanctioning the economic exchange of women's bodies in the wider context of the social reproduction of sexual and social inequalities.

The second alternative approach is a specifically feminist, woman-centred approach as outlined earlier in this chapter. This would acknowledge the lived relations of sex workers' lives and create the intellectual and practical space for their voices and concerns to be heard. The central participation of women working as prostitutes is crucial to this approach. Multi-agency working groups operating at local, regional and national levels, which have sex workers involved as key agents, could develop strategies based around resistance and empowerment. Such strategies located within longer-term goals of policy change need to address the feminisation of poverty and to question the structure and power of masculinist and controlling state apparatuses. They would also serve to 'feminise' the activities and operation of state power in line with socialist feminist objectives, and facilitate empowerment through education, training, networking and policy review.

Conclusion

In summary, this chapter has attempted to highlight the centrality of violence against women prostitutes, and the reponses to violence against women prostitutes by those agencies working through one multi-agency forum in the East Midlands. It has sought to contextualise this work in a critique of the workings of the masculinist state and the concomitant need to feminise the modern state in line with women-centred objectives. Prostitution has to be theorised and analysed within wider sexual, social, political and economic contexts. This entails understanding the lived relations of women's experiences within the context of their access to material and emotional resources, and within an investigation of the relationship between sex worker, prostitution and the role and power of the state. A feminist analysis of prostitution that is concerned to relate feminist theory to women's lived experience and develop policy-oriented practice (feminist praxis) must be concerned most centrally to challenge, resist and change the policies and practices of a 'masculinist state' (and the assumptions on which they are based) tied to the capitalist accumulation process and underpinned by the 'myth of democratic legitimation'.

Notes

1. My initial access to women working as street sex workers was through a health outreach worker. This involved spending many evenings with the women on-street using an ethnographic research approach (Hammersley and Atkinson, 1988). It also entailed watching women being processed by the magistrates court and talking with women off-street. A central finding was that violence is a far greater risk to these women than is disease. I spoke to twelve women in my initial pilot study, ten on-street

and two in-court. The initial pilot study took three months. After this I made contact with another twenty-five women.

2. 'Sex worker', 'whore' and 'prostitute' are used interchangeably throughout the chapter. Some of the women I spoke with preferred the term 'sex worker', and others preferred 'whore' or 'hooker'.

3. Sylvia Walby in *Theorizing Patriarchy'* (1990) defines the state as follows: 'the state is engaged with gendered political forces, its actions have gender-differentiated effects, and its structure is highly gendered. The state is patriarchal as well as capitalist' (p. 150). Furthermore, she continues, 'the state has a systematic bias towards patriarchal interests in its policies and actions' (p. 21). One key implication of a 'masculinist' state is developed by Walby, citing the work of Hanmer (1978) and Hanmer and Saunders (1984): 'They see men's violence as critical in the maintainance of the oppression of women, and the lack of intervention of the state to prevent it is analysed as being the state's collusion . . . when the lack of intervention of either the criminal justice system or the social welfare branches of the state condemn women to subordination. . . . The state is seen as an 'instrument' of patriarchal domination, its non-intervention part of the logic of the patriarchal system' (pp. 156–7). As Connell (1987) has shown, power is equated with masculinity in our society; women are still guests in the public sphere of work and the dichotomy between public world of work and private world of domesticity (man's world/woman's world) still exists; sexuality is still defined within the heterosexual norm with the concomitant binary oppositions being posed between feminine/masculine and passive/active. State agencies such as the police, social services, welfare departments, employment agencies etc. tend to uphold the ideologies and practices that serve to underpin the workings of the masculinist state.

4. See my paper for the British Sociological Association Conference, 6–9 April 1992, *Prostitution, Ideology and the Structuration of Gender: Towards a Critical Feminist Praxis*, for a fuller analysis of the feminisation of poverty vis a vis female prostitutes. Drawing upon the work of Caroline Glendinning (1987), I explore the relationship between poverty and women's entry into prostitution. Glendinning (1987) claims

that conservative economic and employment policies have hit women in paid work in three ways: they are increasingly vulnerable to redundancy and unemployment; the restructuring of the labour market adversely affects the types of jobs and levels of pay women receive and women's statutory rights are eroded when in work. Add to this the costs of daycare for pre-school children and after-school care, and the emergence of a new and poorer underclass – many of whom are women 'caught in a daily struggle to feed and clothe their families' (Glendinning, 1987: 60) – and one can begin to identify the scope of the problem involved in the 'feminisation of poverty'. Moreover there is a central relationship between this process and state action that has systematically 'rolled back the frontiers of the state in keeping with a neo-liberal strategy' (Walby, 1990: 172) at considerable cost to those women and their families dependent upon welfare provision.

5. Exchange value *vis-à-vis* use value (money for sex) is a way of describing the exchange between the prostitute and her client that is shorn of its 'moral' resonances. On the one hand, it is a matter-of-fact description of the exchange that takes place when women work as sex workers. On the other hand, by using Marx's theory of exchange value as a critical rather than a descriptive concept – that is to say, by revealing the way unlike things are treated as though they were like (exchanging money for using women's bodies as public conveniences) – it illuminates the inequalities and double standards operating in the exchange of money for sex. Accepting as taken-for-granted the exchange of use value for money (that it is acceptable to exchange money for the use of women's bodies) this concept helps to reinforce a way of seeing women's bodies as commodities for male consumption – whether it be as prostitutes on-street, as models in pornographic magazines, or as 'fair game' for sexual taunts, innuendo, bullying and harassment.

6. From personal communication with prostitutes in Britain and Europe.

7. In order to avoid further prosecutions in their home town and/or to avoid high-profile policing, some women move on to other towns and cities to work (displacement). They often assume another name and will then be cautioned under the assumed

name. This process buys time and space to work (from personal communication with a representative of an East Midland vice squad).

Acknowledgement

I am indebted to Karen, Sue, Mo, Joanne, Mandy and Shelley, and to members of the Forum for their commitment to our project. However, the theoretical perspective presented here is my own.

7

Working with Men who Abuse Women and Children

Stella Perrott

Introduction

The focus of this chapter is on the work of the probation service, in the preparation of court reports, parole reports and the statutory supervision of offenders on court orders and parole licence. The chapter will examine the assumptions underlying current theory and practice within the profession in relation to child and woman abuse. It will explore the dilemmas these pose for female probation officers who work with abusers within a male-dominated criminal justice system.

In working with offenders the probation service has to be responsive to the often contradictory demands of a number of groups: society, government, the judiciary, offenders and victims. Both offenders and victims struggle to articulate their views within a highly organised and controlled criminal justice system. The conflicts and tensions that exist between the groups are especially apparent in the area of child sexual abuse, as can be seen from the report of the Cleveland Enquiry (HMSO, 1988). They are no less apparent, but less public, in the case of woman abuse. The probation service's work with perpetrators of woman abuse has thus to be viewed within a wider context that encompasses differing ideologies, policies and values.

Sentencing

During the 1980s there was a hardening of government policy in the UK towards those committing violent or sexual offences. After November 1983 restrictions were placed on parole for individuals serving sentences of over five years for offences involving sex, violence, drugs or arson. In these cases, parole is now granted only in exceptional circumstances or limited to the last few months of sentence (Parole Board, 1991). This, coupled with the increasing length of sentences for violent or sexual offences (Home Office, 1990a), has generally resulted in longer terms of imprisonment and fewer opportunities for parole.

The 1991 Criminal Justice Act and its precursor 'Crime, Justice and Protecting the Public' (Home Office, 1990b) brought from the USA the concept of 'just deserts' in determining sentences. This represented a move towards punishments reflecting the seriousness of the crime and away from seeing each offender as an individual whose offence is viewed within a personal and social context. However, abusive offenders are excluded from this policy, receiving longer sentences in some cases: 'giving the crown court power to give custodial sentences longer than would be justified by the seriousness of the offence to persistent violent and sexual offenders, if this is necessary to protect the public from serious harm' (Home Office, 1990d: 14). The move towards longer sentences appears to reflect concern about sex and violence offences and the criticisms raised about some of the short prison or non-custodial sentences that judges have passed against men who abuse women and children (Prison Reform Trust, 1990). In addition, considerable misgivings have been expressed regarding the consequences of serious offenders being released unsupervised into the community. Such was the case of David Evans who murdered a girl within a few weeks of being released (without supervision on parole) in 1988 from a ten-year sentence for rape. As a result, the Carlisle Committee proposals implemented in the 1991 Criminal

Justice Act ensure that more offenders are supervised on parole for longer periods in the community (HMSO, 1990d).

The majority of participants in the criminal justice system are male: police officers, lawyers and judges. The exceptions to this are probation officers and magistrates of whom approximately 50 per cent are female. Probation officers, however, have only a limited role in the courts and the majority of serious violent offences are dealt with by the crown court. Offences, offenders and victims are generally seen through male eyes and sentencing decisions and comments made by judges in the course of trials reflect this. Thus Mr Justice Russell opined of a rape victim who hitched a lift from her attacker that 'she was guilty of a great deal of contributory negligence' (Ipswich Crown Court, *Guardian*, 6 January 1982) and Mr Justice Popplewell commented of a woman who was murdered by her husband that 'this lady would have tried the patience of a saint' (Birmingham Crown Court, Guardian, 1 August 1991).

Despite the Home Office's *Victims' Charter* (1990c) outlining the rights of victims and the resources available for them, there are no new rights to protect victims from attacks on their character by defendants and their lawyers in open court, nor to prevent the details of their ordeal being circulated among offenders in prison by way of the depositions. The 1991 Criminal Justice Act also failed to protect children from having to appear in court and give lengthy evidence under cross-examination. Given that at the same time essential services for victims of violence, such as women's refuges, Rape Crisis Centres and other resources are under threat through lack of funds, it would appear that this more punitive climate reflects a growing antipathy towards sex and violent offenders rather than a desire to help or protect their victims.

The probation officer's role in the sentencing process is to give information to the court regarding an offender's background, current circumstances, attitude to offence and likely response to various sentencing disposals. Most court reports conclude with a proposal for a particular sentence that reflects the seriousness of the offence and the sentence the officer believes may reduce the risk of further offending. The preparation of a report thus provides an opportunity to challenge gender-laden interpretations of the behaviour of both offenders and victims. Such interpretations are common: for example, it is still the case that a girl's previous sexual experience and 'attempts at seduction' are considered by courts to be factors mitigating the seriousness of the offence according to the Court of Appeal guidelines on incest (*Guardian*, 4 August 1989). Unfortunately, many court reports serve to perpetuate gender stereotypes rather than challenge them, particularly when commenting on the extent to which defendants conform to traditional family or female roles (Eaton, 1985).

Some probation officers in their reports have begun to challenge the assumption that a particular offence is an isolated incident. Such officers may express the view that the rape of a child within the family is likely to have been preceded by months or years of preparatory abuse and they may outline ways in which offenders pose risks to other women or children in the future. Such challenges, however, are difficult to make. Harper has noted that social workers in child abuse cases have their work 'dissected in minute detail in public by eminent barristers, skilled in the art of cross-examination which contributes further to the feelings of guilt and inadequacy', and that as a result 'the process becomes a trial of the professionals' (1991: 20). Probation officers can also be questioned or criticised by barristers in court if their reports do not collude with minimising offences or victim blaming. To offer a different explanation of offending or to challenge a defendant's story with the risk of provoking conflict with defence barristers (and possibly judges) takes courage and requires considerable support from colleagues and management. Neither may be forthcoming. It is not surprising therefore that 'the same (feminist) workers are still engaged in work reinforcing various forms of social control of women' (Dominelli and McLeod, 1989: 125).

Probation officers may also attempt to challenge defendants' accounts of their actions and expressed beliefs about their behaviour in the course of supervision. Defendants frequently maintain that the victim 'asked for/deserved/ enjoyed/initiated' the offence (Scully, 1990). The myths are difficult to challenge in the course of work with offenders and doubly so when an offender feels his actions have been endorsed by a trial judge. To say that a woman's behaviour would 'try the patience of a saint' is to suggest that killing her is in some way 'only' human; talk of 'contributory negligence' displaces the blame for the offence on to the victim. In such cases, where probation officers are faced with the task of confronting the offender with the seriousness of his offence, they are likely to have much less credibility than the judge, particularly if they are women.

Diversion

In 1984 the Home Office produced its *Statement of National Objectives and Priorities for the Probation Service*. The first priority was 'to ensure that, whenever possible, offenders can be dealt with at the level required for this purpose' (Home Office, 1984: 5). Following this, most probation services reaffirmed their commitment to supervising high-risk offenders in the community and this has remained central to probation practice. Since the implementation of the 1992 Criminal Justice Act, probation officers are expected in their court reports to outline ways in which offenders can be punished through community sentences, which involve programmes of supervision to prevent reoffending.

Given that 50 per cent of males reoffend within two years of being released from custody (Home Office, 1990d) imprisonment is viewed by the majority of probation officers as a largely negative experience. Most sex offenders are kept on 'Rule 43' (segregation) for the duration of their sentence, keeping only the company of other sex offenders and having plenty of time to fantasise about future offending on release. In 1991 the government proposed new treatment regimes for sex offenders in twenty prisons. These were to include work on victim awareness, deviant arousal (*sic*), interpersonal relationships, communication skills and anger and stress management. These are not yet fully operationalised and apply to only fourteen prisons. There is thus little work being routinely undertaken with sex or violent offenders in prison, and imprisonment may continue to increase the risk of further offending on release: 'Paedophiles in particular tend to congregate in groups. They often swap addresses and units can be the breeding ground for sex rings' (Prison Reform Trust, 1990: 15).

Although probation officers may wish to work with offenders in the community, they frequently lack the effective intervention programmes necessary to reduce the likelihood of reoffending. Many staff are not well trained or equipped to deal with these offences and will not feel confident that they can reduce the risk of reoffending any more than can the prisons (Clarkin, 1988). In addition, many officers may consider that a non-custodial disposal reduces the seriousness with which an offence is viewed by the court and may feel uncomfortable with their role in proposing a probation order. The preparation of a well-argued diversionary report that leads to a shorter or non-custodial sentence will present a conflict for many feminist probation officers. They may feel angry that the offence has not received the sentence that it 'deserved' and concerned about the part their report may have played. A short sentence could mean that a family has little opportunity to establish a way of life without the abuser before his return to the community.

In addition to diversion from custody, diversion from prosecution has also been viewed as a laudable target for the probation service. Considerable work has been devoted to this growing area of practice since the Association of Chief Officers of Probation (ACOP) produced their report entitled *Diversion and Effectiveness* in 1990. Some probation areas have developed schemes to increase the cautioning rates of adults and the discontinuance of criminal proceedings in consultation with the Crown Prosecution Service (CPS) through Public Interest Case Assessment schemes (PICA).

The Women's Aid Federations (Scottish Women's Aid, 1991), Horley (1990a) and others, however, have expressed concern that diversion schemes could be seen to minimise the seriousness of woman abuse:

> The message that society regards violence against women in the home as entirely unacceptable is not yet universally understood and, until it is, decisions to divert violent men will still be confusing and ambiguous (Scottish Women's Aid, 1991: 23).

Diversion from prosecution does not have a long history in respect of adult offenders and, like diversion from custody, poses dilemmas for feminist probation officers. Many domestic violence offences such as criminal damage are not immediately identifiable as such and offenders are frequently charged with less serious offences if the police think they are unlikely to gain convictions on more serious ones (Bourlett, 1990). A man may be charged with breaching the peace, for example, when his actions have resulted in a terrifying experience for his female partner. It is difficult for probation officers to argue for prosecution in such cases when their central aim is diversion. Given the current vogue for diversion, there is a danger that managers will tend to support group work programmes for violent men not on the basis of crime prevention or victim support, but as part of a diversionary 'package'.

Supervision and treatment of perpetrators

The purpose of supervision is:
  - protection of the public;
  - prevention of re-offending;
  - successful reintegration of offenders in the community (Home Office, 1990d: 35).

In working with male perpetrators on probation or parole, the probation officer is required to assist with any practical or welfare problems that arise and consider how best s/he might prevent further offending. However, in her study of work with sex offenders, Clarkin (1988) notes that structured offence-focused work was rare and that practical problem-solving was the primary focus for intervention. Some officers viewed the offence as a 'one off', although there was little evidence to support this judgement.

A 'Women in NAPO' (National Association of Probation Officers) conference in 1988 drew together a number of women working in a variety of settings with men who were violent towards women. The discussions echoed many of Clarkin's findings in that officers felt poorly trained and supported in their work with sex and violent offenders. It was also felt that women, in undertaking offence-focused work, had more of a vested interest in preventing further offending against women and children and that male officers frequently colluded with offenders in discussion of their offences. The potential for collusion is further developed by Dominelli (1988) and has also been recognised by a number of male and female officers (Burnham *et al.*, 1990).

Androcentric theories of woman and child abuse such as those propounded by Freud, Storr, Lorenz and others find many adherents within the probation service. Freud argued that many of his female patients imagined they had been abused by their fathers and that 'a conscious fear is often the expression of an unconscious wish' (Brown, 1964: 19). Similarly, Storr maintained that 'the idea of being borne off by a . . . male who will wreak his sexual will upon his helpless victim has universal appeal to the female sex' (Storr, 1968: 60). Lorenz (1966) added to these gendered assumptions the notion of male aggression as a response to a build-up of pressure that has not found a vent.

The continued acceptance of these theories as an explanation for men's violence is commented on by Brown:

Freudian theory appeared to be saying things that we had known all along . . . that the protestations of innocence or pacific propensities are frequently made by those in whom one suspects the reverse and no amount of criticism from the scientific psychologist is going to make him think otherwise (Brown, 1964: 192).

In other words, Freud and others are believed because they reinforce the view of the 'man' in the street. Such victim blaming effectively diverts attentiom from men's behaviour and the lack of control they exercise over it. These views are given expression through work with clients that focuses on the behaviour of female partners rather than on the behaviour of the abuser.

Although studies by Wyre (1986) and Scully (1990) have shown that victim-blaming theories are inadequate in terms of explaining male violence, probation officers continue to explore marital/adult heterosexual relationships with offenders in seeking explanations for their offending. A study of workers' attitudes to child sexual abuse found that out of forty-two respondents (twenty-five were probation officers), only four did not attribute sexual abuse to individual psychopathy or relationship problems (*NAPO Journal*, September 1989). Not surprisingly, many offenders continue to excuse their behaviour through their partner's lack of sexual appetite.

In focused work with offenders, learning theory has been accepted by many as a significant explanation of child and woman abuse (Renvoize, 1982: Finkelhor, 1984; Miller, 1987). However, in acknowledging the fact that many abusers were themselves abused, there is the danger that we fail to address the issues of individual responsibility and choice. Scully (1990) casts doubt on the explanation that many rapists were themselves abused as children, and the theory fails to explain why women rarely abuse children and are the victims of heterosexual partner murder in almost 75 per cent of cases

(Cameron and Frazer, 1987). Cameron and Frazer also noted that, regardless of the sex of the abuser, men who went on to murder following these experiences invariably chose women as their victims. They argue that men who were abused by their fathers or saw their father abuse their mother would be more likely to be violent towards men were it not for boys' identification with male role models, reinforced and supported by all they meet outside the home. In addition, the widespread use of rape as a means of woman control during periods of slavery or war (Brownmiller, 1975) would indicate that something more systematic than individual experience is at work here.

To fail to address the issues of masculine behaviour and the use of a penis or a fist as a means of woman and child control when working with offenders, effectively colludes with men who believe they have a right to control and dominate women. Furthermore, exploration of a perpetrator's own experience of abuse can often serve to divert blame and responsibility from the abuser and reinforce the belief that he, rather than the child or woman, is in fact the victim. Learning theories, while able to influence therapeutic programmes that work towards changing behaviour, may thus lead to displacement of the problem. The abuser may learn to fantasise about sex with adults rather than children and may still engage in abusive sex with others or in non-sexually abusive behaviour towards children. Therapeutic programmes that are based on learning theories are able, however, to address the influence of the media and pornography and challenge some of the abusive behaviour that may be viewed as normal by offenders (Cowburn, 1990).

In the USA there are estimated to be between 200 and 400 treatment centres for child sex abusers alone, the majority of which charge for treatment – although some are run by 'not for profit' companies (Bentley and Clark, 1989). In view of the government's commitment to the extension of private-sector involvement in the criminal justice system (Home Office,

1990b), this may be the way in which facilities will be developed in the UK in the future. Towards the end of the 1980s offence-focused work with sex offenders received more attention. Community-based treatment programmes were developed and the majority of probation areas began to run programmes for sex offenders based on models of intervention developed by the Gracewell Clinic in Birmingham (Inter-departmental Group on Child Abuse, 1992). These concentrate on the recognition of harm done to those abused and on the development of strategies to avoid further abuse. The Home Office research on the effect of these programmes is not yet complete.

A feminist approach

Feminists view woman and child abuse as an extension of the social construction of masculinity, whereby male power over women and children is maintained. A feminist model for probation intervention addresses the issues of power and gender and approaches the work from the perspective that abuse is a product of societal (male) norms, not individual pathology. Tackling offenders' views of women, control and sexuality is a priority in this work. As with many new approaches to probation practice, the development of sex offender provision has come about through the commitment of individual practitioners who have frequently worked without managerial support or resources to develop initiatives (HMSO, 1991). Service managers are now however beginning to address the work undertaken with abusers. It will be interesting to see if a feminist approach, which has characterised much of the new work to date, will find acceptance in future treatment programmes, given that the majority of senior managers are white men who reinforce a system and culture that works to their advantage (Dominelli and McLeod, 1989; Coulshed, 1990).

According to the 'Index of Probation Projects' for the years 1988–90 there were no projects that dealt specifically with wife abuse – although there were a number of 'anger control' courses for clients. Such courses deal with violence in a general way, using social-skills methods of intervention, and are not designed to deal with violence that arises from, and is legitimated by, the general oppression of one group by another: that is, racist and sexist violence. Many probation officers feel that it is difficult to obtain resources for work that would benefit women, even if it corresponded with the service objectives of increased prevention. It seems that there are plenty of projects nationally that deal with social problems such as unemployment, alcohol and accommodation, but very few that address the issue of violence against women or children (NPRIE, 1990). Although this may be because of lack of commitment from main grade staff, it is also a result of lack of support and direction by managers. Publications such as *Probation in the Community* (Harding, 1987), *New Approaches to Crime in the 1990s* (Locke, 1990) and *Probation Practice in Crime Prevention* (Geraghty, 1991) indicate quite clearly the priority the service and the Home Office has given to young male and predominantly white offenders whose offences are mainly property-related.

The issue of race is also insufficiently acknowledged. Racist responses from the police, housing officials, social workers and others may make it very difficult for black women to leave a violent relationship (Mama, 1989). Whitehouse (1986) noted that when writing social inquiry reports probation officers portrayed black people in a stereotypical way, especially in relation to sexual relationships – typically suggesting promiscuity. Smart (1985) found similar attitudes among magistrates. Thus black women may be especially likely to be blamed for the violence they experience and work with perpetrators by probation officers may serve to minimise the impact of abuse on these women.

Trans-racial sexual violence is a particular area of difficulty for black and white women alike. White women have shown a reluctance to tackle racist assumptions about trans-racial violence in so far as challenging these assumptions may imply they are condoning a violent act. Such dilemmas were present in the debates around the case of the 'Central Park Jogger' (New York) rape trial in 1990 and the Cardiff 'Ripper' (Wales) trial in 1990. In both cases, black men have been convicted of raping white women following what appear to be racially motivated unsafe convictions (Smith, 1990). Davis argues:

> If Black women have been conspicuously absent from the ranks of the contemporary anti-rape movement, it may be due, in part, to that movement's indifferent posture towards the frame-up rape charges as an incitement to racist aggression (1982: 173).

Black women may be reluctant to work with white women on tackling male violence as long as white women effectively condone a racist criminal justice system by their silence. There has been little debate about these issues by feminists working in the criminal justice system in Great Britain. In the 1988 'Women in NAPO' conference on working with abusers, for example, the issue of racism was not addressed; the focus being predominantly on the experience of white women. Although probation services are beginning to tackle racism, the service as a whole is a long way from developing effective anti-racist practice.

Alongside the prevention of reoffending through offence-focused work, the probation service aims to help offenders reintegrate into their communities on release from custody. Frequently this means returning 'home' and this can raise many conflicts. Although child abusers may be pressured to stay away from children, the same process does not apply to woman abusers: the latter may be actively encouraged in their attempts to resume existing relationships or form new ones. This is particularly the case to the extent that a settled life-style is thought to be a factor in preventing reoffending and having a 'good home' to return to is more likely to lead to a favourable parole result (Parole Board, 1991). To discourage a violent man from returning home when both parties agree to his return, even in the knowledge that further abuse is inevitable, is a difficult task and to describe the home circumstances as 'unsuitable' in a parole report may lead to considerable dissent from both partners.

Working with perpetrators

Casework evidence gained through my involvement with 'Women in NAPO' indicates that many women staff experience considerable tensions in working with abusers. Many managers appear to deal fairly unsympathetically with female staff who express concerns about this kind of work. Some female probation officers who have themselves been abused have been required to work with abusers (immediately after being vaginally and anally raped in one case). They have received comments like: 'It will help you get over it' and 'We all have to be professional about these things'. In one case reported to us, an officer was instructed to continue working with a man who had threatened to rape her. Not all managers are unsympathetic, but many female officers feel reluctant to discuss their personal experiences, especially ones of abuse, with people who ultimately decide whether they are good enough to do their job or to achieve promotion.

As many have noted, working with sexual abuse is stressful (O'Hagan, 1989; Dominelli, 1988), and yet officers and social workers have little opportunity to share with others the effect the work has on them. It is difficult to discuss these anxieties in mixed support groups, especially if they relate to intimate relationships with other people. Moreover, many officers are now required to work jointly, but may be allowed little choice over their working partners. Feminist workers in particular are unlikely to feel comfortable in discussing sexual matters with an offender alongside a colleague who does not share their view of child or female sexuality. The truth of Germaine

Greer's famous phrase 'Women have very little idea of how much men hate them' (1971: 249) comes only slowly to those who work with abusers, and they may rarely be able to acknowledge this with male colleagues.

When working with abusers, female officers may become the subject of a man's sexual or violent fantasies. The offender may continually try to undermine them with phrases such as 'if you were my wife' or 'if you were raped'. Women working with groups of abusers, even when working with male probation officers, sometimes find themselves as the sole defender of women and children, continually being expected to explain the female (as if there was only one) perspective. Male clients may resent female probation officers who are in a position of authority, and if the officer is both black and female the resentment may be greater (see Chapter 5 in this volume). Abuse of physical power and a wish to dominate may be expressed by abusers in their relationships with female officers. They may view their probation officer as the next victim or gain pleasure from eliciting fear or unease. Discussion of the depositions for the preparation of a report or work on the offence may be enjoyed by an offender as an opportunity to relive his experiences. It will be a difficult and perhaps distressing experience for both female and male workers and, if they do not feel in control of the interview, they may feel victimised by this experience (Moore, 1990).

Conclusion

Working with offenders who are violent towards women or children poses many dilemmas for probation officers. Undertaking the work is in itself a compromise for many feminists who believe it is a male problem that should be resolved by men. In working with offenders, staff may be expected to pursue an approach that is in conflict with their beliefs about the causes of offending. There may be little support or training available, and even less that encourages an anti-sexist and anti-racist practice. There is little evidence to suggest that challenging masculinity is a priority for the probation service and feminists working within the service are likely to feel that the problems they face are not recognised or acknowledged as valid.

Developing feminist practice with abusers

Many probation officers, both male and female, wish to develop an anti-sexist approach to work with abusers and much of the group and individual work that has been developed in recent years is a reflection of this. Probation officers working in a male-dominated criminal justice system and with a male-dominated probation service management will not find it easy to take on a campaigning role in relation to work with abusers. Considerable work, however, can be undertaken in this area through local NAPO branches, Women in NAPO, ACOP and our links with other organisations at local level. There is much that can be done to develop a feminist approach to the work and the following principles should underpin our activities in this area of practice:

Campaigning issues

- Groups for men should not be set up and funded at the expense of facilities for abused women and children, and such groups should only operate in areas where there are adequate resources for women and children.
- Partner abuse is a serious crime and not suitable for diversion from court alongside minor offences such as shoplifting.
- Any reduction in local-authority services that penalises women and children, i.e. the funding of refuges and Rape Crisis Centres, should be challenged.
- We should support social services colleagues in Cleveland, Nottingham and elsewhere when female professionals are

accused of 'breaking up families' when trying to expose the extent and effects of child abuse.

- We should work with local women's groups that are struggling to be heard above the clamour of male 'expert' voices.

Management issues

- All staff working with sex and violent offenders should have appropriate training in anti-sexist and anti-racist practice.
- In-service support groups should be encouraged, with a facility for women-only groups. All supervisory staff should receive training that will enable them to support staff in their work with abusers.
- Officers should be able to 'opt in' to work with perpetrators rather than be compelled to do so.

Probation practice

- Probation officers should address the issues of gender and power in their work with abusers, both at an individual and societal level.
- When preparing reports for court or the parole board, we should not lend our authority to the excuses men give for abuse and, in cases where these are likely to be put forward in mitigation by lawyers, we should ensure that our reports do not give credence to their arguments.
- When arguing for non-custodial sentences, our reasons should reflect the paramountcy of victim protection and plans to address offending behaviour should be clear and unequivocal.
- In child protection cases, our understanding of the abuser should be shared with social services in order to help them in their role. It should be made clear to the abuser from the outset that any relevant information will be shared.

- We should examine all aspects of probation practice that involve work with abusers, i.e. anger control courses, sex offender groups and individual work, and ensure that the programmes are run on anti-sexist and anti-racist lines.

8

Violence Against Social Services Staff: A Gendered Issue

Marianne Hester

In the past couple of decades, largely as a result of the women's movement, men's violence to women and children has been made increasingly public. This has been accompanied by a recognition that violence may be used as a means of social control by those with power over those with less power. As feminists, we have – quite understandably – spent less time examining violence to those in positions of power, be they men or women. Yet feminist analysis must provide an understanding of this area as well.

Following a number of violent attacks on social workers in Britain over the past decade, violence to social services staff has become a public issue. There has been a heightened awareness of violence at work and the establishment of guidelines for dealing with violent incidents by many social services departments (SSDs) (Johnson, 1988). It has been recognised that social work is an occupation where violence (at least from clients to staff) is likely to occur, and perhaps increasingly so (Small, 1987; Sharron, 1985; Schulz, 1987; King, 1989). This is because, although deemed a 'caring profession', social work can involve the taking of individuals' personal liberty, as in compulsory admission to psychiatric hospital and accommodating children in care. Staff may be perceived by clients to be taking a 'policing' rather than a 'caring' role, and staff themselves may feel this contradiction:

. . . it is a system that actually doesn't operate any more, in terms of finances and what have you. [The clients] were after demanding things and I think they thought that social workers sit there and give out all sorts of stuff, and when I didn't, Father erupted (Hester and Florence, 1990).

Many staff end up seeing some level of violence as 'part of the job' with which, as individuals, they are expected to cope.

In this chapter I look at violence to social services staff who, as professionals, may be in a position of relative power over their clients, but who, especially as female workers, may also be in a less powerful position in relation to colleagues and possibly male clients. There are two main issues I want to address as crucial to our understanding of violence in social work. The centrality of sex/gender in relations of violence is one of these issues; in the present patriarchal context, women's experience of violence may differ significantly from that of men (Hester, 1992). The other issue is how the experience social services staff have of violence to themselves informs their professional practice with clients who have experienced violence.

Other issues of power, such as authority or positioning in the social services hierarchy and race, are also important. I will consider the question of authority, but am unable to consider race in any depth at this stage because most of the studies in the area of violence to social services staff unfortunately omit this issue. The work undertaken by myself and Penny Florence was carried out in a social services department with an almost exclusively white staff group. Nonetheless, there is evidence that issues of race and ethnicity, such as racial harassment of black staff, are central to the issues of violence at work (see Bryan, Dadzie and Scafe, 1985; Bhavnani, 1988; Jowell and Airey, 1984; Brown, 1984).

This chapter examines recent research into the nature and frequency of violence experienced by social services staff 'on the job', and draws on interviews with these staff carried out during 1989 and 1990 (Hester and Florence, 1990) in addition to other relevant studies and material.

Sex/gender and research into violence in social work

Since the late 1970s a number of studies concerning violence in
social work have been carried out in Britain: Brown, Bute and
Ford (1986), Crane (1986), Rowett (1986), King (1989) and
Saunders (1987). The studies tend to focus on violence to
social workers from clients and consider to varying degrees the
effect of male–female relations on the context and nature of
violent incidents. Some, such as Crane and King, ignore the
issue of sex/gender entirely. As far as the definition of
'violence' is concerned, these studies mainly concentrate on
physical rather than other forms of violence, and conclude
that male social workers are more likely to be subject to such
violence than female staff. This chapter will question whether
the use of such restricted definitions may exclude important
areas of experience. In particular, it will question whether a
focus on physical violence gives primacy to men's experience
of violence above that of women's.

Race tends not to be considered at all. In the one study that
does mention race, it is only the 'race/nationality' of the clients
that is noted (Rowett, 1986: 86), thus giving the impression
that race and nationality (other than white British) are
features of the 'violent client' – rather than part of the
structural power dynamic between staff and clients.

One of the earliest large-scale studies was that of Brown,
Bute and Ford (1986), who administered a non-random postal
questionnaire to 560 SSD staff in Wessex, and received replies
from 60 per cent of the recipients. The sample was obtained by
contacting relevant professional organisations. It included
fieldwork, residential and day care staff, but excluded others
such as receptionists – even though the authors recognise that
'as "front line" workers they are affected by many of the same
issues as the respondents' (1986: 2). Brown *et al.* suggest that
those who responded to the questionnaire were possibly more
likely to have experienced violence than a comparable random
sample, but they emphasise that the level of violence indicated
by the survey was none the less higher than expected.

Unfortunately they do not say what forms the basis of this expectation.

The definition of violence used in Brown *et al.*'s study was 'actual physical assault resulting in some injury or pain' (p. 1). On the basis of this narrow definition they found that day care workers were the group most likely to experience violence (50 per cent), followed by residential workers (45 per cent), and then fieldworkers (22 per cent) (p. 4). Within these categories it was male workers who were proportionately more likely to experience violence, and who were likely to experience more than one incident. These distinctions apply only to day-care and residential staff as the study did not consider sex/gender with regard to incidents of violence among fieldworkers. In general, it concludes that: 'men working in close contact with clients in day centres are the most likely group to be assaulted, and some priority should be accorded to dealing with the problem' (Brown, Bute and Ford, 1986: 18).

Rowett (1986) carried out one of the most extensive studies of violence to social workers, conducted at three levels: a national postal survey of all local authority SSDs; a scanning questionnaire to all social workers in one Shire County Department; and structured interviews with a sample of social workers from the Shire County scanning population, of whom half had been assaulted and half had apparently not been. About two-thirds of the respondents were women (66 per cent of the field social workers and 69 per cent of residential social workers). Rowett argues that those assaulted were more prepared to be interviewed, the self-selected sample thus tending to overrepresent those who categorise themselves as having experienced assault. I would want to add, however, that it may also underrepresent the actual level of assaults.

Individuals' own level of (stated) awareness of violence should be treated as a problem within this area of research insofar as it may influence what respondents perceive to be relevant aspects of their experience. Feminists have recognised how, without a specific 'name' or label, it is very difficult to articulate experience (Dworkin, 1981); and, in the patriarchal context within which we live, it is largely men's experience that has this means of articulation. I would suggest that this validation of men's experience may lead men to take part more readily in the studies outlined, and be more able or willing to talk about their experiences of violence.

Rowett's study looks at violent incidents to social workers with direct client contact, including unqualified social work staff but specifically excluding other staff. He points out, quite rightly, that the way 'violence" is defined will influence the outcome of research, but nonetheless goes on to use a restricted definition where ' "violence" refers only to physical violence resulting in actual physical harm to the social worker' (1986: 30). Threats and abuse, or any other form of emotional or psychological violence, are excluded – although some respondents pointed out that the psychological effects of violent injury may be at least as damaging as the physical components. While he included 'sexual violence' within his definition, his failure to find any violence within this category is related to his failure to present it to respondents as a separate category. Our research suggests that it is important to separate out as many different categories of violence as possible (see also Saunders, 1987). Rowett used a card-sorting exercise to elicit perception regarding violence, finding that 'no-one considered sexual assault to a be a likely occurrence' (1986: 115). What he does not acknowledge, however, is that in the case of sexual violence the perception of what constitutes violence may be far removed from the actual rate of its occurrence (Kelly, 1988; Hanmer and Saunders, 1984).

The scanning survey had a response rate of 62 per cent – similar to the response obtained by Brown, Bute and Ford in their more selectively distributed questionnaire. Echoing Brown *et al.*'s findings, Rowett's survey also suggests that assaulted social workers are more likely to be male and working in a residential setting.[1] Rowett finds the emphasis on male workers particularly difficult to explain, as there is nothing in his scanning data to provide such explanation. He does not consider the possibility that men may be more likely to report violence, nor whether this discrepancy is an effect of the definition used.

Rowett's interviews bring to the fore further questions related to gender. Focusing on the sex of the clients who had assaulted social workers, Rowett finds overall that 'male and female social workers were as likely to be attacked by clients of the opposite sex as by those of the same sex' (1986: 87). Though, taking field or residential setting into account as well, he indicates that residential social workers were more likely to be assaulted by male clients, and field social workers by female clients. He suggests the reason for this distinction is, for the former, the greater number of adolescent males in residential care with a history of violence; and, with regard to the latter, more families with children in care, as well as women with a mental health problem, being dealt with by field staff. He finds it difficult, however, to explain his finding that no female field social worker in his sample had been attacked by a male client, beyond attributing this to the small number of female social workers in the sample as a whole. Again, Rowett's use of a somewhat restricted definition of what constitutes violence may also prevent him from considering whether female workers are experiencing other forms of violence in such situations – for example, verbal violence or threat of violence. The one distinction he does appear to make is that, while more men appear to be assaulted overall, women are more likely to be assaulted repeatedly and 'proportionately more frequently' than men (1986: 127). Although it is not clear exactly what he means by this, it seems to imply that a few women become ongoing victims of violence.

A broader approach

Saunders's study of violence to staff in Surrey SSD (1987) builds on Rowett's work, but is distinguishable in two ways. First, it uses a much broader definition of violence that includes the categories: physical assault, physical abuse, sexual assault, sexual abuse, threat, property damage or theft, and 'other' forms not contained elsewhere. Secondly, the survey includes all types of staff, from clerical through to managerial grades, deemed to be 'front line staff and their managers or supervisors' (1987: 32). The study consists of a scanning questionnaire, a follow-up questionnaire to those indicating they had experienced violence and were willing to be questioned further about their experience, and personal interviews with a small sample.

The scanning questionnaire was sent to 4055 members of staff, all of whom had direct contact with the public or who managed or supervised such staff. The response rate (39 per cent) was much lower than in the case of Brown *et al.* and Rowett, but included a much higher proportion of women respondents: with 88 per cent women and 12 per cent male. The response rate from managers and professional staff was especially high, and these individuals, according to the survey, also experienced more violence. This reinforces the findings of Rowett and also by Brown *et al.*, although the latter's staff groups were more restricted. Overall, Saunders's scanning survey suggests that violence is widespread and more prevalent than is often thought – occurring within all workbases, in all types of job, to all age groups and both sexes – and with over a third of the respondents having experienced it in some form.

Taking Saunders's results from the scanning questionnaire first, she found, as did the other studies mentioned above, that residential staff are more likely than fieldwork staff to experience violence. With regard to gender there is also a similarity in the general finding that men are more likely than women to experience violence in any setting. A new finding, however, concerns sexual violence and sexual abuse, where Saunders found that the risk to both sexes is equal. This finding is notably different from that obtained by the questionnaire and interview stages of her research, and also different from much research on sexual harassment at work (see Russell, 1984; MacKinnon, 1979).

Only 49 per cent of those responding to the initial scanning questionnaire who had experienced violence were prepared to be questioned further about their experience. Saunders queries this poor response, suggesting that the climate for discussing the issue of violence is perhaps not as open as it might be – a point made by many feminists (Hanmer and Saunders, 1984; Kelly, 1988; Stanko, 1985). The individuals who were willing to respond were sent one questionnaire for each of the seven types of violence identified. It is interesting to note that the greatest number of questionnaires sent out related to the category of 'threat', followed in terms of quantity by the categories of 'physical abuse', 'physical assault', 'property damage or theft', 'other', 'sexual abuse' and 'sexual assault'. The categories of sexual abuse and sexual assault were particularly small.

In contrast to both Rowett's and Brown *et al.*'s work, most of the workers replying to Saunders's questionnaire were women – at least within both the physical abuse/assault and sexual abuse/assault categories. Consequently, for Saunders the largest number experiencing violence is also women – although her work suggests, as do the earlier studies, that proportionately men are more likely to experience physical violence. What stands out from this approach, therefore, is that the use of a series of separate categories of violence (plus questionnaires) enabled more people, and especially women, to perceive their experiences as 'violence'.

Saunders's categories of sexual abuse and sexual assault provide some particularly interesting results where sex/gender are concerned. Only one individual, a woman, reported an incident clearly relevant to the 'sexual assault' category, but placed it under the category 'other'. In other words, she did not directly define her experience as sexual assault. Regarding sexual abuse, twelve staff reported a total of thirty-six incidents over a period of five years. These were mainly instances of female workers abused by male clients, 'although one female and one male worker were abused by a woman' (Saunders, 1987: 46), presumably a client. Also, staff who had been sexually abused reported that 83 per cent of incidents had had an adverse effect on their work practice – twice the effect compared with any other form of violence experienced (p. 48).

Use of 'threat' as a separate category is another departure by Saunders from earlier studies. Others have pointed out the importance of examining the effect of threat to social services staff, but not much study of this has otherwise been made (Bute, 1979; Small, 1987). Saunders found that the threat 'of death or of actual bodily harm' was the most common, and was reported by men about twice as often as by women (p. 46). The largest number of questionnaires was returned within this category, and the adverse effect on staff's work practice was at the same level as that for physical assault and physical abuse.

The Exeter study

Our small-scale study on violence in social work in the South West, undertaken in 1989–90, grew out of an extensive training project designed to help social services staff deal with violence at work, primarily from clients but also from colleagues. When the research began, about one hundred members of staff had already attended the courses, and it became apparent that violence was being defined very narrowly to mean mainly extreme physical violence. At the same time the staff's experiences of other forms of violence – verbal, emotional and sexual – were being minimised and often obscured. I wanted to build on the previous research and also to move beyond this by adopting a qualitative approach informed by feminist work into violence against women (Hanmer and Saunders, 1984; Kelly, 1988; Stanko, 1985; Mahony, 1985; Duelli Klein, 1983; Du Bois, 1983). This has found that individuals may be more able to talk openly about their experience of violence in a context that includes dialogue, where their experience can be taken seriously and shown to be relevant. In such a context women especially may be more able to 'name' their experience as violence, and as a particular form of violence. A qualitative approach (such as semi-structured interviews) is more likely to reveal a realistic picture of both the nature and frequency of violent incidents than a quantitative one.[2]

In order to establish a better picture of the frequency of violent incidents we took a representative sample of staff throughout the organisation: from clerical through to managerial levels. Interviewees were selected by means of a random sample of those who had attended a 'Violence at Work' course during 1988–9. We knew they had recently discussed the issue of violence, and had had a chance to examine their own experience. These included whole teams, groups of reception and clerical staff, and staff chosen to attend the course on the basis of a variety of criteria such as being newly appointed, being team leader, or being available on that day.

Twenty-one staff were contacted, sixteen women and five men, all of whom agreed to be interviewed. There were eight social workers, two senior family centre workers, two family centre workers, two part-time family centre workers, and one of each of the following: records' clerk, under fives' worker, assistant social worker, assistant officer, deputy principal officer, principal officer, and family centre manager. Thus within this small sample there was representation from most levels of the Department, although with an emphasis on children's services.

The interviews were conducted on the following areas: the nature and level of incidents, context, monitoring, and training. We found that the best approach involved the use of a generally open and flexible interviewing technique, yet with highly structured options on the different forms of violence. This allowed the fullest extent of violence, especially that against women, incidents of a sexual nature, and the significance of sex/gender to be brought to the fore. We separated out the different forms of violence into the categories of 'actual verbal', 'actual physical', 'actual sexual', 'verbal threat', 'physical threat', 'sexual threat', and looked at its occurrence over two periods: the previous twelve months and the period before that time.

It is not possible to make statistically valid generalisations from such a small sample, but the results from the study nonetheless provide useful indicative data. Within the sample, men had experienced an average of four violent incidents and women three incidents over a comparable period. In this sense the study appears to echo the general findings of the studies outlined earlier. What is interesting here, however, is the willingness of individuals to take part in the study. While all agreed to participate, the five men agreed readily, whereas some of the women required a fair degree of persuasion. This was not because they did not think it important, but because they did not think they had any relevant experience. In the event, only one woman had no direct experience of violence in any form. She was a clerical worker, and even she had observed two violent incidents at the office.

This undervaluing of women's experience (by themselves, let alone others) was notable at other points during the research and forms one of the obvious distinctions between men and women in the sample. It may be a factor affecting the different number of incidents reported by men and women, such that women are under-reporting in comparison with men. In addition, some women interviewees (more so than men) appeared to be blocking questions, either consciously or unconsciously. One striking instance was that of a woman who came to her interview very well prepared, with notes and files, but who could not properly remember what she had wanted to say and interspersed her responses with expressions of dissatisfaction at what she was saying.

The Exeter study echoed the earlier findings that men were more likely to experience actual physical violence than women. Discussing this phenomenon, Small suggests that the reason 'may be that male workers adopt more threatening stances and so contribute to an escalation of violence or it may be that situations that look as if they may include violence are more often allocated to male workers' (Small, 1987: 43). We also found that men are much more likely to become involved in a violent incident not initially directed at them, possibly escalating the violence or bringing it upon themselves in this way.

Women, on the other hand, are more likely to experience both verbal and sexual abuse rather than physical abuse. Where sexual violence is concerned, three women talked about specific incidents, one man said he had experienced sexual violence, and other workers talked more generally about the problems of such violence. As found by others (Kelly, 1988), it was often necessary to take time to establish greater confidence between interviewer and interviewee with regard to sexual violence than with other types of incidents. This issue has apparently not been taken into account in the previous studies on violence to social services staff. Sexual violence is especially likely to be seen as something which, as one worker put it, 'you do not scream round the office'; female staff may find it difficult to get the occurrence of sexual violence either believed or taken seriously by colleagues.

One woman talked about the unsupportive reaction she had received from other staff after a boy in a family centre had repeatedly attempted to 'get her into compromising situations'. She recalled how everyone, staff and clients, had laughed at first. Yet another female member of staff, who had been sexually harassed over a period of five years by a colleague, said that 'a lot of abuse goes on that's unnoticed – and even where it is recognised, you're not allowed to admit it'. When she finally reported what was happening to her, it was implied that she was part of the problem, having 'brought it on herself'. She tried to direct the man towards help, but colleagues implied she had been wrong to do so and deserved what she got. 'What she got' included actions she described as 'psychological violence, verbal violence and threats' in addition to sexual advances and intimidation.

Women's apparent undervaluing, minimising or denial of their own experiences should be considered in the light of this as examples of how women tend more often to end up being blamed for the violence directed towards them, especially if it involves sexual violence. Overall, it is questionable whether the amount of violence to male social services staff is actually much greater than that directed at female staff. It is important to explore whether female staff are instead experiencing different forms of violence such as sexual or verbal abuse – forms of violence that may be more difficult to either talk about or record than physical violence.

Violence and professional practice

Our study indicates that the perceptions social services staff have about the nature and occurrence of violent incidents are often in contradiction to their own or colleagues' actual experiences. Beliefs about, for instance, men's and women's different roles and authority play a part in this. Moreover, the staff often see the violence they themselves experience in quite a different way to the way they see that which is experienced by clients.

The frequency and extent of violence experienced by staff interviewed in our study and the other studies outlined earlier might lead one to think that they would expect violence, or consider it a likely occurrence. However, the effect of this 'context of violence' is actually to restrict both male and female staff's view of what does constitute violence, and to minimise what has happened to them. This is reflected in the way many social services staff see their roles and leads them to accept a certain level of violence as 'normal'. Indeed, staff interviewed as part of this project often commented that violence 'Happens all the time', 'It's a daily occurrence', and that it is all part of the job. Despite this, nearly all said that they themselves did not expect to experience violence. Saunders's findings echo this (1987).[3]

During the 'Violence at Work' courses, many staff talked about their reluctance to report violent incidents. They felt there was a general assumption within the organisation that if you were good at your job you would not face violence, and they wanted to defend their professional standing. As one male member of staff commented, violence may be more threatening to social workers 'as you question your ability to deal with it'. But clearly, the reluctance of members of staff to anticipate or expect violence is also a part of their coping or survival strategy, as well as a defence of their professionalism. One woman, who had herself been abused as a child, linked the expectation of violence to a victim role, a role she no longer saw herself in. Another explained that she did not expect violence, but focused on being able to handle the situation. Interestingly, one worker, who was herself experiencing sexual harassment at work, commented that she expected verbal abuse, but not physical or sexual violence.

While the majority of the staff did not themselves expect violence, they thought on the other hand that their clients did expect violence. Staff commented, for instance, that 'it is part of [clients'] lives', 'part of the norm', that 'it is their short sharp solution to their problems'. Women and children in particular were considered likely to expect violence. Clearly, some clients are in touch with social services partly because they are perceived to be violent, or because they live in an abusive situation. What is more important, however, is the way the staff, despite their own experience of violence, made distinctions between their expectation of violence and that of clients: while clients live in a violent, and openly violent, (sub)culture, social services staff do not. I would suggest rather that clients, just like social services staff, may be minimising and 'normalising' their experience of violence and may therefore not come to expect it even if they regularly experience it.

When asked about possible differences or similarities between their own experience of violence and that of clients, about half the staff interviewed suggested that their experiences differed, and the other half talked about similarities. One senior member of staff explained how she thought her experience of violence was different to that of clients. Violence from clients was not actually aimed at her, but at the organisation. She therefore did not take it personally, and found this was an effective means of minimising its impact.

Those members of staff who thought there were similarities between their own experience of violence and that of clients often focused on the emotions involved, and were more likely to have experienced abuse, either sexual or physical, as children. For instance: 'similar to own experience of battering as a child', 'feel the same – flight and fright', 'takes you right back, remember sick feeling and despising self', and 'yes, same emotions: violation, humiliation, a reducer'. These staff appeared more able to empathise with clients and to calm down a potentially violent situation.

Interviewees were asked whether they felt gender had made (or would make) any difference within any incident that they actually had experienced. In other words, if it mattered whether they were male or female. Responses were often contradictory. A number of individuals said that women are more likely to defuse situations than men, but it was also suggested that women are not authoritative enough to cope in violent situations. When asked whether an incident would have been any different if he had been a woman, a male social worker replied that he was at first aided by 'his perceived authority as a male'. 'This would not have been there had I been a woman', he remarked. In other words, he thought a woman would be less able to contain the violence. Another worker, a senior member of staff, talked fluently about the differences between boys and girls, but repeatedly qualified her remarks with observations that tended to minimise the importance of gender: 'Depends on the case, depends on the client'. Yet sex/gender was clearly an important aspect. One female family centre worker, for instance, found she could work easily with girls, but that the boys attempted to undermine her through verbal abuse.

Conclusion

Violence to social services staff is a widespread phenomenon, and takes all forms: physical, sexual, verbal and psychological, from clients as well as from other staff. Crucial to our understanding of such violence is that the violence experienced is related to sex/gender, as is denial or minimisation of that experience. Thus male staff are more likely to face physical violence, female staff sexual and verbal violence; and women are less likely to talk about their experiences or to have them recognised by other members of staff.

With regard to perception, staff tend to expect less violence than they think clients expect. Staff see themselves as working within a culture that is less violent than that of clients. This may lead staff to see clients' lives as quite distinct from their own, and reduce their ability to relate directly to clients' experience. In short, it leads them to erect barriers of 'professionalism' between themselves and clients. Yet, when staff do take their own experiences of violence (within or outside work) into account, they are often more able to understand the context, process and effect of the violence that their clients experience.

A number of issues appear particularly important if practice concerning violence at work is to be improved, including awareness building and the development of accessible procedures and support systems for staff. In particular:

- Violence needs to be acknowledged and taken seriously if staff are to be able to talk about and have validated the incidents they experience. This is especially important with regard to women, since not only do women make up the bulk of social work staff, but it is their experiences that are more likely to be ignored or devalued.
- The many different forms of violence (in addition to physical assault) need to be taken into account, including sexual, verbal and psychological abuse.

- There has to be a focus in training and supervision on the similarities and links between staff and clients' experiences of violence to enable staff to increase their understanding of the process and effect of violence. Violence cannot necessarily be avoided, but this will help staff minimise the possibility of violence.
- Support in the form of debriefing or counselling should be easily available to staff who have been subject to violence (Braithwaite, 1989).

Notes

1. Included within Rowett's category of 'residential setting' is the category of 'day care' as used by Brown, Bute and Ford (1986).
2. In their recent study of frequency of abuse in a sample of 16–21-year-olds, Kelly, Regan and Burton (1991) have very successfully used a large quantitative approach to elicit details of incidents. However, this approach was informed and made possible by previous qualitative work carried out in a way that set out to validate and take seriously the experiences of the respondents.
3. We may, of course, question whether social services staff should be expected to accept violence as a normal part of their jobs.

Acknowledgements

I want to thank Penny Florence for her work on the Exeter research, and our many useful discussions about the results. Also, I am grateful to my Department at Exeter for providing a grant to carry out the study.

9

Violent Women

Joan Orme

. . . to fight has been the man's habit, not the woman's. Law and practice have developed that difference whether innate or accidental (Woolf, 1977: 9).

Introduction

In a feminist text on women, violence and the response of the public services it is essential that there is an account of violent women. Although the numbers of such women appear to be small, reactions to them tend to be disproportionately strong, and negatively influence their treatment, especially within the public services. In providing an account of violent women, this chapter examines the gendered assumptions of violent behaviour, and explores the extent to which these have led to the differential treatment of such women. The chapter argues that one group of violent women, those who kill, provide a clear example of the consequences of such gendered assumptions about violent behaviour. Such women serve as a salutory postscript to the rest of this book. Women who kill are most often those with no history of violent behaviour, but who have resorted to killing after prolonged abuse from male partners. The circumstances in which they kill, the perception of their behaviour and the standards against which they are judged, illustrate key issues relating to the treatment of all violent women.

Such an analysis is necessary because, to date, two central strands have emerged from the literature on violence and women. The first is the classic, and traditionally male, set of studies that present an analysis of aggressive or violent behaviour as a positive and natural drive to be condoned, at least when demonstrated by white males (Lorenz, 1966; Storr, 1968). Such an analysis either ignores female violence or ascribes negative connotations to it. The second is the literature from the feminist movement that importantly and correctly has focused on male violence against women (Pizzey, 1974; Brownmiller, 1975; Hanmer and Maynard, 1987; Wilson, 1983).[1] What has been conspicuously absent from both perspectives, until very recently, is the consideration of women who are violent – that is, those who will resort to the use of physical abuse/force, with or without the use of a weapon. This may be because the number of such women who come to the attention of the public through the criminal justice system or the mental health services is small. These women are a source of conflict and confusion for both perspectives.

The fact that there is an apparent difference in the level of violent behaviour of women and men has led to an exploration of the causes of this difference. As with so many analyses of female behaviour, there is an historical dimension. Traditional theories have been expounded by males: male behaviour has been taken as the norm and women's behaviour has been defined in relation to that norm. Such theories have been challenged in a number of ways by feminist thinkers, and there has been a growing sense that male definitions, methodologies and criteria do not have to be accepted as substantive (Stanley, 1990). Feminists have accordingly sought to define and explain female behaviour in its own right and not as relative to the male, arguing that the experiences of the few are as meaningful as those of the many. As Segal claims, 'contemporary feminists have also emphasised that "the political" is more than collective actions and campaigns in the public world. The personal and subjective struggle of all oppressed people is one against being defined as inferior, marginal and deviant, in the language, discourse, myths and fantasies of the dominant culture' (Segal, 1987: xi).

Increasingly, this has meant that the definition or categorisation of women had similarly to be challenged. Within the use of the terms 'female' and 'woman', there is a wealth of different sets of behaviours, social and economic circumstances, and ethnic and cultural backgrounds that have equal validity.

Women are violent

The acknowledgement that women are violent presents a challenge to some of the accepted theories of female behaviour. For traditional male theorists the assumption that 'aggression in females is only fully aroused in response to threat, especially if the young are involved' (Storr, 1968: 86) becomes untenable as not all women convicted of acts of violence commit such acts in defence. Indeed, a particular group of violent women – mothers who physically abuse their young – present a pattern of behaviour that is directly contradictory to Storr's assumption. It may well be that this contradiction contributes to the strength of feeling against such acts. For feminist theorists, the analysis is more interestingly complex. Some would not want to perpetuate the myth that it is necessarily 'unfeminine' to be aggressive, because in general they would eschew such definitions. Nevertheless, female violence does contradict the philosophy, embodied in what Segal (1987) has called 'cultural feminism' and personified by the women of Greenham Common, that women, either by constitution or history, are non-violent and that they have the facility to change situations without recourse to the use of force or violence. The fact of female violence therefore contains a central paradox. This is identified by Campbell who acknowledges that 'whilst it [feminism] has reinterpreted women's behaviour it has sometimes shared stereotypes of femininity rather than challenged them. It has often reproduced a picture of women as victims, life givers rather than life takers, peacemakers rather than warriors' (1991: xiii). Many black feminists would confirm this view. To say that violence is essentially masculine denies the experience of black people at the hands of white women, and the involvement of black women in violent resistance to white oppression (Bhavnani, 1987).

That girls can be violent is illustrated by Campbell's study (1981) of working-class girls, which found that 89 per cent had been involved in a physical fight; and by Robins's (1984) study of football hooliganism, where girls were found to be just as likely to join in the fighting on the terraces. That women commit offences of violence, and that the number of such offences is on the increase, is supported by the information in the *British Crime Survey*. In 1986, 7 per cent of all female crime involved offences of violence, but by 1990 this figure had risen to 10 per cent. This survey also gives some information about the nature of women's violent offences because, while women have contributed to all types of crimes of violence in the 1980s, they are responsible for less than 10 per cent of all murders and the majority of their convictions are for wounding (HMSO, 1991a).

There are of course a number of explanations for the rise in the figures for offences of female violence. The first suggests that women are committing more acts of violence. This may be true, but on the basis of these figures we cannot automatically make such an assumption. The figures may reflect a change in attitude towards women who are violent. Within the criminal justice system there are opportunities for diversion from prosecution at a number of points and there is evidence that these opportunities are used differentially. For example, in 1989, 31 per cent of women over the age of 21 who were apprehended for offences never appeared before a court and instead received a caution, while only 13 per cent of males in the same age group were cautioned. It may be that women who committed acts of violence in the late 1970s were more likely to be diverted into, for example, the mental health services than in the 1980s. If, on the one hand, the figures reflect a growing willingness to prosecute, then this may suggest an acceptance on behalf of police, prosecutors and sentencers that women do have the potential to be violent. On the other hand, if those in the criminal justice system are continuing to divert, then the increase in female crime may be greater than these statistics suggest.

Whatever the cause of the increase in the statistics, it is the assumptions and attitudes underpinning the response to them that have consequences for all women. The most significant of these is that because not many women are seen to be violent (and it is accepted that even if there was a consistent treatment of the sexes within the criminal justice system there may still be more instances of male violence), then it is 'natural' or 'innate' for women to be non-violent. Thus women are being judged against a set of standards based on male norms which leads to certain consequences in their treatment by the public services. Such treatment involves the pathologising of violent women, their systematic diversion into the mental health services, or inappropriate intervention in their personal lives by the 'caring' professions. Before exploring such processes in detail, it is first necessary to consider the explanations of female violent behaviour that have informed them.

Explanations of female violence

Biologism

Storr has argued that 'the biological difference in both quality and quantity of male and female aggressiveness implies that they are not interchangeable. There is a biologically appropriate way for males to be aggressive and another for the female' (1968: 86).[2] The consequence of these assumptions is that women who behave in a biologically inappropriate way, by showing physical violence, are deemed to be abnormal and dealt with accordingly. This approach involves the reduction of all behaviour to its biological basis. Storr was not alone in the 1970s in taking a biologistic view of behaviour. Maccoby and Jacklin (1974) similarly claimed that the more aggressive behaviour of males was innate. The critique of this approach by Archer and Lloyd (1982) and Sayers (1986) highlights the limitations of sample sizes and the practice of extrapolating from research on animals to explanations of human behaviour. Levitas challenges the biologism of Storr and others on the basis that they confuse 'the biological categories of sex with the social categories of gender' (1983: 123). She suggests that any argument that propounds the 'naturalness' of a particular personality characteristic or trait on the basis of biological inheritance is suspect because 'attempts to calculate the degree of heritability of a trait, such as intelligence or aggression (that is trying to decide "how much" is due to heredity and how much to environment) are misguided; the conditions necessary for the statistical tests are not, and cannot, be met'. In terms of female aggressiveness, therefore, it is not possible to devise a measure that could accurately determine whether such behaviour was 'biologically appropriate'.

For our purposes, the need to counter the assumption that women are innately non-aggressive is essential because one of the outcomes of a description of behaviour as biological, genetic or hereditary is the 'legitimating force of the term "natural"' (Levitas, 1983: 120). The effect of this argument can be seen in the way that violently aggressive behaviour in women is so frequently perceived as being 'unnatural' and defined in terms of madness. It is this that often leads to their differential treatment within the criminal justice system and to specific outcomes when dealing with violent women in other parts of the personal social services.

Medicalisation

One of the direct consequences of biologism has been an attempt to find a rationale, or excuse, for those women who appear to be acting in an unfeminine or unnatural way. The initial reaction is to look to women's physiology for a possible cause. Hence the use of concepts such as premenstrual syndrome to explain the behaviour of women who commit acts of violence. This approach labels women who conform to societal norms of female behaviour as healthy and those who do not as in some way ill. Luckhaus (1985) points out that there are a number of instances where women have received differential treatment under the law on the strength of a defence argument for premenstrual tension (PMT), but the consequences of such a verdict are not always in women's best interests. Even though women may receive a reduced sentence, they have had to accept definitions of themselves such as having 'diminished responsibility'. Agnes Buchan, for example, was placed on probation for a period of three years for the killing of a man who attacked her friend. In admitting to manslaughter, Mrs Buchan was described as being 'in an excited and volatile state because of PMT' (*Guardian*, 30 July 1991). In some cases, the sentences have been described as lenient, but Luckhaus warns that women who use PMT as a mitigating excuse are vulnerable to the vagaries of individualised sentencing and can be detained in mental hospitals or be the subject of restriction orders. In these circumstances, the length of the detention becomes indeterminate and the 'leniency' might lead to a longer period of incarceration. Women using the defence of PMT may also be subject to compulsory medical treatment.[3]

Similar assumptions about women's biology operated in the framing of legislation such as the 1938 Infanticide Act. This reflects a reluctance to accept that a woman would kill a child without there being a physiological reason – in this case, the belief that, because of hormonal imbalance post-childbirth, a woman is not responsible for her actions. Although not directly related to acts of violence, the concept of the 'menopausal shoplifter' similarly reflects a description of women as being victim to what de Beauvoir calls the '"hysterical body", in the sense that there is, so to speak, no distance between the psychic life and its physiological realisation' (1972: 356). This closeness of the psychic with the physiological and the connection between the 'endocrine secretions and the nervous and sympathetic systems that control the muscles and the viscera' mean for de Beauvoir that a woman's body 'displays reactions for which the woman denies responsibility; in sobs, vomiting convulsions, it escapes her control, it betrays her' (1972: 630).

This is a very powerful process whereby a woman, because of her physical constitution, is reduced to a particular set of physiological circumstances that cause her to behave in an aberrant way. Such reductionism 'impugns the integrity of the female actor, stripping her action of cultural and political meaning and anaesthetizing the social and political origin and conditions in which her action takes place' (Luckhaus, 1985: 177). The contradiction is that most women experience both menstruation and the menopause, but not all women commit violent acts while they are doing so. In seeking to medicalise the behaviour of some women there is an invocation of the normal experiences of women leading to abnormal behaviour. Such arguments have implications for the women who commit the acts of violence, but also contribute to the continued oppression of women generally, because they perpetuate the view of them as irrational and emotional beings subject to the unpredictability of their hormones. The logic behind the process of medicalisation is that if a woman's behaviour is challenging the accepted norms then there must be something distinguishable about that woman, not that the norms are based on false assumptions.

Pathologising or psychiatrisation

The next most powerful labelling process that occurs for violent women is that of pathologising or psychiatrising. There is no attempt to seek the explanation for the behaviour in the social, political or economic context of that woman, or to accept that she was 'just mad with anger'. The solution is that she was 'just mad'! Such explanations presume that at the time of committing the act of violence the woman was in a disturbed state of mind. As Allen found in her research, offences of maternal violence were 'routinely attributed to psychiatric disorder' (1987: 102). Other behaviours that are seen to require a psychiatric explanation and that attempt to place the rationale for the action within the personal pathology of the woman rather than in her social circumstances, are those where women do not conform to gendered stereotypes. Hence black women and lesbian women are perceived as behaving in ways that both attract negative labelling and lead to assumptions about their mental instability because they deviate from the assumed norm of a white heterosexual woman who is defined in terms of home, family and partner.

Worral (1990) describes this as 'the gender contract', where the discourses of law, medicine and psychiatry converge to assume that 'being a normal woman means coping, caring, nurturing and sacrificing self interest to the needs of others. On the other hand it is characterized by lack of control and dependence' (p. 35). It is when women conform to this norm that courts will act with chivalry, and suggest that the sentence should not necessarily fit the crime: that a woman should not necessarily receive her 'just deserts', but rather needs the protection of the court and the intervention of the caring professions.

Such interpretations can have two effects. First, there is precipitative intervention by agencies such as the probation service and a hastening of girls and women up the sentencing tariff. Hence acts of violence that might be perceived as being 'high spirits' when committed by boys, are seen as representative of problems which require intervention when committed by girls and women. Probation orders that are subsequently breached mean that custodial sentences are given to women who have committed fewer and less serious offences. In other respects this chivalry is more lenient to women. Allen argues that they are more likely to get the supportive community-based intervention of the psychiatric services than their male counterparts. She further argues that, although some women have repeatedly committed offences of violence, there is a reluctance to accept that they are a threat to the public. 'The woman is presented as "deprived", "damaged", "victimised", and "insecure"' (1987: 101).

Edwards (1986) argues, however, that this 'sick' model of women's violent behaviour does not always operate to their advantage. Her research indicates that they are likely to be given a comparatively longer prison sentence, held in special conditions such as 'H wing' at Durham jail, or be subjected to treatment plans such as the use of behaviour-modifying drugs. As Edwards comments, 'where the defendant does not conform to conventional crime patterns and her gender behaviour is at variance with acceptable patterns of female domesticity, of family and home centredness, she is frequently regarded as dangerous, in need of custody or even containment in a secure mental hospital' (1986: 80). Furthermore, if women continue to challenge the accepted norm of compliance, if they react violently to the environment in which they are placed, then they are moved on to special hospitals. Here they may suffer from chronic lack of staff and become subject to indeterminate sentences (Stevenson, 1989).

Some men who commit violent offences may receive similar sentences, but there is no automatic assumption behind such sentencing that men who commit violent offences are at best acting in an 'unnatural' way and at worst are mad. The difference is that for men, unless they are black, most of the sentencing decisions consider all aspects of their situation, with each being given equal weight, free of any underlying negative assumptions or stereotypes. Indeed, sometimes acts of male violence appear to be condoned, or at least assumed to be explicable. This is illustrated by situations where men have been found guilty of wife assault, but whose sentences are reduced because their violence is perceived as 'understandable' in the face of the female who 'nags', or threatens his sexuality by her 'infidelities'.

Socialisation

Counter to the biological determinist model and the medicalisation response is the approach that argues that differences in behaviour are the result of socialisation: 'determined by children's and adults' understanding of sex and gender, and by the rewards associated with gender conformity' (Sayers, 1986: 11). Thus it is possible to argue that female violence is not necessarily unnatural or abnormal behaviour. The purpose here is not to prove that women are as aggressive as men nor that we would wish them to become so, but that the differential levels of violent aggressiveness are as much to do with the socialisation of both sexes as they are to do with any innate personality characteristics. As de Beauvoir argues, 'it remains true that her physical weakness does not permit woman to learn the lessons of violence; but if she could assert herself through her body and face the world in some other fashion, this deficiency would be easily compensated for' (1972: 357).

It is possible to accept the studies cited by Storr that identify differential levels of violence in nursery school children (1968), but to argue that, even at this stage, gender role stereotypes are already in operation. Girls are aggressive, they do fight, but the acceptability of this often relates to the circumstances. As Sharpe suggests, it is legitimised in the 'sporty toughness found in girls' boarding schools where it is popular and acceptable, and also in the activities of gangs of young working class girls which have developed in other schools' (1976: 71). What is significant for our purposes is the reactions to such behaviour. These are that it is 'unladylike', unfeminine and abnormal. The distinctions are even more extreme than this because, as Sharpe points out, the differences between boys and girls are monitored and commented on from a very early age, if not pre-birth. Behaviour is constantly stereotyped. To be active, assertive and aggressive as a girl is to be labelled as a 'tomboy', carrying with it a mixture of positive and negative connotations (Archer and Lloyd, 1982). For a boy to display gentleness and caring is to earn the label 'sissy' or, in the language of the 1990s, a 'girl' – a term of contempt and derision.[4]

A further analysis of the process of socialisation is offered by French (1986), who suggests that aggressiveness is learned in a culture where certain sets of values predominate: a culture that 'worships power, individuality, disconnection from others, and competition; and disparages the satisfactions of life devoted to affection, fellowship and harmony' (p. 561). More particularly, this learning is gender-based. Societies have fostered aggressiveness in males to prepare them to go to war, women are discouraged from participating in war because they are needed to reproduce the nation. The argument that men learn to assert their aggressiveness in more violent ways than women is part of the social mediation referred to by Levitas, and is argued equally strongly by Morgan (1987), who points to the legitimation embodied in parades and national ceremonies, in mythologies and stories. He also suggests that male violence is further legitimised by the normalisation of small boys' play. Such legitimation of male violence is germane to this chapter because it raises the possibility of a similar legitimation of female violence. If such a legitimation was available, it would help us to argue for an acknowledgement of female violence without the pejorative assumptions of 'madness or badness'. As Morgan points out, 'one consequence of this [normalisation] is the denial of legitimacy for violence when carried out by women' (1987: 184).

Here we have the rub: that aggressive behaviour, when demonstrated by white heterosexual males, is under certain conditions understandable (if not excusable) but not when the perpetrators are female, and/or black, and/or homosexual. Hence when seemingly 'normal' women, those in heterosexual relationships, commit the ultimate violent act of killing their partner, the public services react strongly. It is the treatment of these women who commit acts of violence in the domestic arena that compares so unfavourably with that of men who have committed acts of 'domestic violence'.

Women who kill

The consequences of violence perpetrated by men and women are often related to the physical differences that cause them to take particular forms of action. These differences are related to size and strength. Women do not always act spontaneously in threatening situations because of fear of being overwhelmed. Also, women in relationships operate within a whole series of mechanisms that prevent them from taking the offensive. They will often excuse their partners and defend them to the extent of blaming themselves for the behaviour (Cline and Spender, 1987). This analysis can be a direct consequence of accepting the notion of the superiority of women's non-aggression (Segal, 1991). The denial of the capacity to be violent often leads to the turning of the aggression inwards and subsequent depression within the woman. It also perpetuates the projection of all the power and violence on to the male and establishes male violent behaviour as normal.

This is reflected in the criterion for the legal defence of provocation in domestic disputes, where crimes of violence are measured against the 'reasonable man' test (Edwards, 1985). This yardstick for acts of violence that lead to the death of a victim means the difference between a conviction for murder or manslaughter. To date, a conviction for murder means a mandatory life sentence. Hence women may be sent to prison for life for acts of violence in circumstances where men who argue provocation may receive much more lenient sentences. The conditions for a conviction for manslaughter are that the perpetrator has to demonstrate that s/he acted as any 'reasonable man' would have done; that the amount of violence was proportionate to the perceived threat, and that the danger was imminent. Women's actions frequently arise out of expressions of incapacity and helplessness rather than an exercise of power. There may in fact be little difference from the motivation of some men, but the interpretations of the actions are different and these interpretations lead to assumptions of premeditation.

The reality for women is that either through constitution or circumstance they are not likely to act as a 'reasonable man'. When threatened with violence, when subject to continual oppression and acts of aggression, they are unlikely to feel able to retaliate physically. However, when their tolerance breaks, when they finally commit an act of violence in circumstances designed to minimise the possibility of violent retaliation, they are presumed to have acted with premeditation because their victim may have been drunk or asleep at the time. Jones's study of women who kill identified how, in situations of wife assault, sentencers assumed that 'the alleged passivity and helplessness of battered women is better understood as lying low – an active, venerable, temporary and smart survival strategy' (Jones, 1991: 363).

Two examples serve to illustrate the dilemma for women who kill. Their behaviour has been mediated by a variety of circumstances that cause them to act in a particular way. However, that action is, as described above, set against tests that are not informed by an acknowledgement of the way that female behaviour is framed. The second aspect of the dilemma is that this lack of acknowledgement causes them to resort to explanations of their behaviour that perpetuates the very processes that, it has been argued, have militated against women generally.

In 1991 Sarah Thornton lost her appeal against a life sentence for the murder of her husband. She had been married for just over a year when she stabbed her husband after he had returned home drunk, mocked her and threatened to kill her and her child. He was an acknowledged alcoholic and had made repeated threats against her and her daughter by a previous marriage. At her trial, Sarah Thornton's defence was one of diminished responsibility on the grounds of her personality disorder. She had to give details of the time she had spent in a psychiatric hospital some nine years previously. Thus she had to present herself as mad, and no weight was given to the fact that her husband had attended a clinic for alcoholism much more recently. The plea was not accepted, and in July 1991 she appealed on the grounds of provocation because she had been the victim of systematic violence.

During the same period, Karanjit Ahluwalia was also convicted for the murder of her husband after ten years of violence, threats and degradation. She had made attempts to escape, had taken out injunctions against him and had appealed to the police for help, but was also subject to the influences of her family and her culture which persuaded her to make her marriage work (see Chapter 4 in this volume). Two hours after a particularly vicious beating and a hot iron pressed against her face, she threw petrol at her husband's feet while he was asleep, 'just enough for him to know what it was like to feel pain' (*Spare Rib*, 1990). This action led to his death. At her trial, the defence failed to submit all the evidence that might have constituted a defence on the basis of provocation. Instead, it tried to prove she only intended grievous bodily harm. She was convicted of murder and sentenced to the mandatory life imprisonment and remained in prison until September 1992 when, at a retrial, she pleaded guilty to manslaughter on grounds of diminished responsibility and was then released.

There are differences in these cases, not least that, for a variety of reasons, these two women had very different advice at the time of their trials. With the support of a black feminist pressure group (Southall Black Sisters), Karanjit began to prepare her case for appeal, but ironically did not receive attention in the daily press until the case of a white woman, Sarah Thornton, was publicised. The plea on the grounds of diminished responsibility was recommended by a psychiatrist who diagnosed Karanjit as suffering from 'endogenous depression'. Southall Black Sisters, while recognising that it is wrong that women have to use medical reasons and claim diminished responsibility for an act that was directly provoked by years of violent behaviour and abuse, nevertheless saw the adjudication as a turning point.

A political campaign is being fought to change the British law along the lines of that in the USA, where premeditation can be accepted in acts of domestic violence, but does not automatically incur a mandatory life sentence. The decision in the Karanjit case acknowledged that provocation can build up over a period of time and that women do not have to act like a 'reasonable man'. While such a campaign is taking place, there are other issues to do with the daily practice of those who work with violent women that need to be addressed.

Challenges to practice

The explanations of violent behaviour in women and the acknowledgement of the differential treatment by both the criminal justice system and the psychiatric services lead to a number of dilemmas for, and challenges to, those involved in working in the public services.

The first challenge is directly related to the notion of femininity or appropriate female behaviour, and the reaction of those in positions of authority to those who fail to conform to such notions. If we are to influence the response to violent women, it is not a question of operating only at the level of the personal or the institutional. It is a matter of both. The probation officer preparing the social inquiry report has to resist the temptation to assess the individual offender, whatever the sex, in terms of role, race or class stereotypes. It is no more acceptable to describe an offence of male violence as being the norm for a particular community than it is to emphasise the differences from the norm in female behaviour. Nor should those in the psychiatric services condone the attitudes that define mental health in terms of behaviour that is socially accepted and gender specific, such as performing housework or wearing make-up to attract or please male partners.

At the point of intervention or sentence it is difficult not to be influenced by the knowledge that the presentation of women as conforming to white heterosexual norms may influence the outcome. Hence in social inquiry reports of probation officers or assessments of social workers the pressure to excuse or to explain in order to achieve a more desirable outcome is difficult to resist (see Chapter 7 in this volume). However, as Allen argues, 'the struggle for women's equality will never be furthered by the attempt to retain either the privilege or the disabilities of femininity' (1987: 120). But what are the alternatives? Should social workers advise lesbian and black women, who rightly want to express their anger at the continual oppression they have suffered at the hands of the system because of their 'deviance' from the norm, to curb their anger and act submissively in order to receive a less severe sentence? The National Association of Probation Officers has issued guidelines (NAPO, 1990) to assist its members in acting in a non-sexist way. These recommend that probation officers should *not* resort to stereotypical definitions and biological explanations of female behaviour, and recommend a system of gatekeeping reports to ensure that language and descriptions are monitored.

However, there is a real dilemma in using the most vulnerable and powerless women as a vehicle for educating decision-makers. Such women have to be given the choice. They have to be informed of all the possible consequences and it is for them to indicate how they want to proceed. This in itself is fraught with difficulties. Can women such as Karanjit really be expected to refuse a plea of mitigation on the grounds of 'endogenous depression' if to do so might lead to a continuation of a life sentence?

Such difficulties occur because we are constantly trying to define and even excuse women's behaviour against a predominantly male norm. If it is accepted that women are violent and that violence may be directly related to the circumstances in which the act occurred, then there may be less emphasis on the abnormal and less discrepancy in the treatment of such women. The consequences are twofold. First, in identifying that women do commit violent acts there is a responsibility for those dealing with them to accept that this is so for a number of reasons, and to assess and accept them according to criteria that are not to do with stereotypical assumptions about behaviour or life-style. Second, if women have the capacity to be violent, but have been socialised to be non-violent, then that process can operate for men. At both a personal and organisational level there is a need to legitimate the activities of both males and females which concern acceptance, co-operation and caring.

The question is, how do we achieve this? Segal's suggestion that 'we could simply feed men regular doses of oestrogen, or perhaps merely the huge quantities of valium which women are currently swallowing to curb men's aggression' (1987: 181), carries with it all the criticisms of intervention that assumes that all behaviour is biologically based. The responsibility lies rather with individuals and institutions within society that are responsible for monitoring and responding to human behaviour. They need to enable men to unlearn the violent ways, and to validate the non-violent ways. This is in marked contrast to a value system in which a public service such as the police force, through the Home Office, produces a document in response to violent crime that consists of a catalogue of ways in which women must curtail their personal freedom in order to protect themselves against male violence (HMSO, 1987). It is a reflection both of the power of feminist action and the part-acceptance of the socialisation argument that a subsequent document (HMSO, 1990) contained suggestions for ways in which men could behave in less threatening ways.

Here we are entering into the arena of public policy, and the impact of policy on practice. If it is accepted that women have the potential to be violent and that violence is, for some women, a reaction to a particular set of circumstances, then there is a responsibility to do something about those circumstances. In America it was documented that, when the number of women's refuges was increased, and women were given more assistance to leave violent and oppressive relationships, the number of murders by women of their partners decreased significantly (Jones, 1991). There is an obvious message for British policy-makers who have consistently underfunded refuges and hostels for battered women.

If we can accept that women have been socialised into behaving in non-violent ways despite their capacity for violence, then we must accept that men too can be socialised into different models of masculinity and that this is an important and legitimate strategy for working with men who have been convicted of acts of violence against women and children. The implications are apparent for all those involved in the public services, and not just those who deal with violent individuals. Those in child care have an opportunity to influence models of parenting behaviour and child-rearing patterns. This does not only mean actively encouraging a greater sharing of the parenting role by both partners, where there are two, but allowing and encouraging the expression of emotions,whatever the sex of the child. It is as acceptable for a boy to cry as it is for a girl to produce a tantrum.

Conclusion

In this chapter we have charted how the statistically low number of women committing acts of violence has been associated with negative assumptions and the unfair differential treatment of these women. Such treatment is based on the normality of male aggressiveness, a normality that keeps women in a state of threat in both their personal and public lives. To reject this notion – to acknowledge that women have the potential to be violent, but have been socialised into non-violent ways – has a twofold effect. The first is that the treatment of those women who are violent will not involve them being labelled as unnatural or mad. The second is that, in acknowledging the potential of socialisation, we can work towards a reversal of the norm. To reject all violence necessarily involves an acceptance that men can be socialised into non-violent ways. Such a change would have implications for the personal and professional practice of us all.

Notes

1. The issue of male violence is implicit in most feminist literature, but there are also specific texts. It is not possible to give a comprehensive list, but early studies tended to be subject related, such as Brownmiller (1975) on rape and Pizzey (1974) on domestic violence, although Wilson (1983) did attempt to address the major issues. More recently the literature has attempted to deal with the underlying causes of violence against women, e.g. Hanmer and Maynard (1987) and French (1986).
2. It could be argued that the date of Storr's text reflects thinking that has been subsequently discredited. However, a revised edition of *Human Aggression* was published in 1992, with no changes in the assumptions about the innateness of female non-violence.
3. In Agnes Buchan's case, it was part of the defence that she was now receiving treatment for PMT.
4. For a more detailed and powerful extension of this argument, see Mary Daly's *Gyn/Ecology* (1984), where she suggests that the male fear of being 'effeminate', or being labelled as such, 'has nothing to do with the reality of living women, but with an awareness on the part of "femininity", or "effeminacy" or "woman" – and which they attempt to exorcise by projecting it upon really existent women as well as women of their fantasies' (p. 360).

References

ACOP (1990) *Diversion and Effectiveness*, Association of Chief Officers of Probation.

Adler, Z. (1991) 'Picking up the Pieces', *Police Review*, 31 May, pp. 1114–5.

Ahmed, S. (1990) *Black Perspectives in Social Work*, Birmingham, Venture Press.

Ahmed, S., Cheetham, J. and Small, J. (1986) *Social Work with Black Children and their Families*, London, Batsford.

Ahrens, L. (1980) 'Battered Women's Refuges: Feminist Cooperatives versus Social Service Institutions', *Radical America*, vol. 14, no. 3, pp. 41–7.

Allen, H. (1987) *Justice Unbalanced*, Milton Keynes, Open University Press.

Anthias, F. and Yuval-Davis, N. (1992) 'Contextualizing Feminism: Gender, Ethnic and Class Divisions, in L. McDowell and R. Pringle (eds), *Defining Women: Social Institutions and Gender Divisions*, Cambridge, Polity Press.

Archer, J. and Lloyd, B. (1982) *Sex and Gender*, Harmondsworth, Penguin.

Armstrong, L. (1990) 'Making an Issue of Incest', in D. Leidhort and J. G. Raymond (eds), *The Sexual Liberals and the Attack on Feminism*, New York, Pergamon Press.

Barrett, M. and McIntosh, M. (1982) *The Anti-Social Family*, London, Verso.

Bart, P. B. (1989) 'Rape as a Paradigm of Sexism in Society – Victimisation and its Discontents', in R. D. Klein and D. L. Steinberg (eds), *Radical Voices*, New York, Pergamon Press.

Bass, E. and Davis, L. (1988) *The Courage to Heal: A Guide for Women Survivors of Sexual Abuse*, New York, Cedar.

BASW (1988) 'The Guide to Policy and Practice in the Management of Child Abuse', *Social Work Today*, vol. 6, no. 10.

Beauvoir, S. de (1972) *The Second Sex*, Harmondsworth, Penguin.

Ben-Zavi, R. and Horsfall, E. (1985) 'Adolescent Rape: The Role of Rape Crisis Counselling', *International Journal of Adolescent Medicine and Health*, vol. 1, nos 3–4, pp. 343–56.

190

Bentley, M. and Clark, P. (1989) *An American Experience*, Greater Manchester Probation Service.

Bentovim, A. and Mrazek, P. B. (1981) 'Incest and the Dysfunctional Family System', in P. B. Mrazek and C. H. Kempe (eds), *Sexually Abused Children and their Families*, Oxford, Pergamon Press.

Bentovim, A. *et al.* (1988a) *Child Sexual Abuse within the Family*, London, Butterworth.

Bentovim, A. *et al.* (eds), (1988b) *Child Sexual Abuse within the Family: Assessment and Treatment*, London, John Wright.

Bhavnani, K. K. (1988) 'Is Violence Masculine? A Black Feminist Perspective', in S. Grewal *et al.*, *Charting the Journey: Writings by Black and Third World Women*, London, Sheba, pp. 263–8.

Bhavnani, Kum Kum (1988) 'Turning the World Upside Down', in S. Grewal *et al.*, *Charting The Journey, Writings by Black and Third World Women*, London, Sheba.

Binney, V. *et al.* (1981) *Leaving Violent Men. A Study of Refuges and Housing for Battered Women*, Leeds, WAFE.

Blagg, H. *et al.* (1988) 'Inter-agency Co-operation: Rhetoric and Reality', in T. Hope and M. Shaw *Inter-Agency Coordination: Rhetoric and Reality*, Home Office Research and Planning Unit, HMSO.

Blair, I. (1985) *Investigating Rape*, Beckenham, Croom Helm.

Blom-Cooper, L. (1985) *A Child in Trust: The Report of the Panel of Inquiry into the Circumstances Surrounding the Death of Jasmine Beckford*, London Borough of Brent.

Borkowski, M., Murch, M. and Walker, V. (1983) *Marital Violence – The Community Responses, London, Tavistock Publications*.

Bourlett, A. B. (1990) *Police Intervention in Marital Violence*, Milton Keynes, Open University Press.

Bourne, J. (1983) 'Towards an Anti-Racist Feminism', Institute of Race Relations, London, *Race and Class*, vol. XXV, 1.

Bourton, A. and Burnham, L. (1989) 'Stand by Your Man or Your Child?', *Community Care*, 14 September.

Boushel, M. and Noakes, S. (1988) 'Islington Social Services: Developing a Policy on Child Sexual Abuse', *Family Secrets: Child Sexual Abuse, Feminist Review*, no. 28, January, pp. 150–7.

Braithwaite, R. (1989) 'Training for Trouble', *Community Care*, no. 773.

Brent CHC (1981) *Black People and the Health Service*, Brent Community Health Council.

Brenton, M. (1985) *The Voluntary Sector in British Social Services*, London, Longman.

Brief (1986) Greater Manchester Police Newsletter, 14 May.

Brook, E. and Davis, A. (1985) *Women, the Family and Social Work*, London, Tavistock Publications.

Brown, C. (1984) *Black and White in Britain*, London, Heinemann.

Brown, J. A. C. (1964) *Freud and the Post-Freudians*, Harmondsworth, Pelican.

Brown, R., Bute, S. and Ford, P. (1986) *Social Workers at Risk*, London, Macmillan.

Brownmiller, S. (1975) *Against Our Will: Men, Women and Rape*, New York, Bantam Books.

Bryan, B. Dadzie, S. and Scafe, S. (1985) *The Heart of the Race – Black Women's Lives in Britain*, London, Virago.

Bureau of Crime Statistics and Research New South Wales (1985) *Sexual Assault Police Evaluation* – Interim report on the pattern of reporting between the police and Sexual Assault Centres.

Burgess, A. and Holstrom, L. (1979) *Rape, Crisis and Recovery*, Bowie, Brady.

Burnham, D. *et al.* (1990) 'Offending and Masculinity: Working with Males', *Probation Journal*, September.

Bute, S. (1979) 'The Threat of Violence in Close Encounters with Clients', *Social Work Today*, vol. 11, no. 14, pp. 12–15.

Butler-Sloss, E. (1988) *Report of the Inquiry into Child Abuse in Cleveland*, London, HMSO.

Cameron, D. and Fraser, E. (1987) *The Lust to Kill*, Cambridge, Polity Press.

Campbell, A. (1981) *Girl Delinquents*, Oxford, Basil Blackwell.

Campbell, B. (1988) *Unofficial Secrets*, London, Virago.

Campbell, B. (1991) Introduction in *Women Who Kill*, London, Gollancz.

Carew-Jones, M. and Watson, H. (1985) *Making the Break – A Practical, Sympathetic and Encouraging Guide for Women Experiencing Violence in their Lives*, Harmondsworth, Penguin.

Carlen, P. (1988) *Women, Crime and Poverty*, Milton Keynes, Open University Press.

Carter, P. *et al.* (1989) *Social Work and Social Welfare Yearbook, 1*, Milton Keynes, Open University Press.

Carter, P. *et al.* (1992) 'Malestream Training? Women, Feminism and Social Work Education', in M. Langan and L. Day (eds), *Women, Oppression and Social Work*, London, Routledge.

Ching Louie, M. (1991) 'Hope for Battered Asians', *New Directions for Women*, vol. 20, no. 2, p. 9.

Clarke, J. and Newman, J. (1992) 'Managing to Survive: Dilemmas of Changing Organisational Forms in the Public Sector', Paper presented to the Social Policy Association Conference, University of Nottingham, July.

Clarkin, L. (1988) *Probation Officers' Practice with Child Sex Offenders*, Northumbria Probation Service.

Clifton, J. (1985) 'Refuges and Self-Help', *Sociological Review Monograph*, no. 31, pp. 40–59.

Cline, S. and Spender, D. (1987) *Reflecting Men at Twice Their Natural Size*, London, André Deutsch.

Collins, C. (1986) *We Want to be Anti-Racist – But We Don't Know What to Do*, London Voluntary Services Council.

Conn, J. and Turner, J. (1990) 'Working with Women in Families', in R.J. Perelberg and A.C. Miller (eds), *Gender and Power in Families*, London, Routledge.

Connell, R.W. (1987) *Gender and Power*, Cambridge, Polity Press.

Corbett, C. and Hobdell, K. (1988) 'Volunteer-based Services to Rape Victims: Some Recent Developments', in M. Maguire and J.H. Pointing (eds), *Victims of Crime: A New Deal?*, Milton Keynes, Open University Press.

Coulshed, V. (1988) *Social Work Practice: An Introduction*, Basingstoke, Macmillan.

Coulshed, V. (1990) *Management in Social Work*, Basingstoke, Macmillan.

Cowburn, M. (1990) 'Assumptions about Sex Offenders', *Probation Journal*, March, pp. 4–9.

Crane, D. (1986) *Violence on Social Workers*, Social Work Monographs, Norwich, University of East Anglia.

Dale, P. *et al.* (1986) *Dangerous Families*, London, Tavistock Publications.

Daly, M. (1984) *Gyn/Ecology*, London, Women's Press.

Davis, A. (1982) *Women, Race and Class*, London, Women's Press.

Davis, A.Y. (1984) *Women, Culture and Politics*, London, Women's Press.

Davis, L. V. (1987) 'Serving Battered Women: A National Study', unpublished thesis.

Delacoste, F. and Alexander, P. (eds) (1988) *Sex Work: Writings by Women in the Sex Industry*, London, Virago.

Dobash, R. E. and Dobash, R. P. (1980) *Violence against Women – A Case Against Patriarchy*, Wells, Open Books.

Dobash, R. E. and Dobash, R. P. (1981) 'The Community Response to Violence Against Wives', *Social Problems*, vol. 28, no. 5, pp. 563–81.

Dobash, R. E. and Dobash, R. P. (1987) 'The Response of the British and American Women's Movement to Violence Against Women', in J. Hanmer and M. Maynard (eds), *Women, Violence and Social Control*, London, Macmillan.

Dobash, R. E. and Dobash, R. P. (1992) *Women, Violence and Social Change*, London, Routledge & Kegan Paul.

Dominelli, L. (1988) *Anti-Racist Social Work*, London, Macmillan.

Dominelli, L. and McLeod, E. (1989) *Feminist Social Work*, Basingstoke, Macmillan.

Drake, R. F and Owens, D. J. (1992) 'Consumer Involvement and the Voluntary Sector in Wales: Breakthrough or Bandwagon?', *Critical Social Policy*, no. 33, vol. 11 (3), pp. 76–86.

Driver, E. and Droisen, A. (1989) *Child Sexual Abuse: Feminist Perspectives*, London, Macmillan.

Droessler, C. (1991) *Women at Work: First European Prostitutes' Congress Reader*, HWG, Federal Republic of Germany.

Du Bois, B. (1983) 'Passionate Scholarship: Notes on Values, Knowing and Method in Feminist Social Science', in G. Bowles and R. Duelli Klein (eds), *Theories of Women's Studies*, London, Routledge & Kegan Paul.

Duddle, M. (1985) 'The Need for Sexual Assault Centres in the United Kingdom', *British Medical Journal*, vol. 290, pp. 771–3.

Duelli Klein, R. (1983) 'How to Do What We Want to Do: Thought about Feminist Methodology', in G. Bowles and R. Duelli Klein (eds), *Theories of Women's Studies*, London, Routledge & Kegan Paul.

Dunhill, C. (ed.) (1989) *The Boys in Blue: Women's Challenge to the Police*, London, Virago.

Dworkin, A. (1981) *Pornography: Men Possessing Women*, London, Women's Press.

Earle, J. (1988) 'Sexual Assault Centres in New South Wales', Pre-meeting paper from the 'Police Response to Rape' National Meeting, London.

Eaton, M. (1985) 'Documenting the Defendant', in J. Brophy and C. Smart (eds), *Women-in Law*, London, Routledge & Kegan Paul.

Edwards, A. (1987) 'Male Violence in Feminist Theory: an analysis of the changing conceptions of sex/gender violence and male dominance', in J. Hanmer and M. Maynard (eds), *Women, Violence and Social Control*, Basingstoke, Macmillan.

Edwards, S. (1986) 'Neither Bad nor Mad: The Female Violent Offender Reassessed', *Women's Studies International Forum*, vol. 9, no. 1.

Edwards, S. (1989) *Policing Domestic Violence – Women, the Law and the State*, London, Sage Publications.

Edwards, S. (ed.) (1985) *Gender, Sex and the Law*, Beckenham, Croom Helm.

Esland, G. (1980) 'Professions and Professionalism', in G. Esland and G. Salaman (eds), *The Politics of Work and Occupations*, Milton Keynes, Open University Press.

Faludi, S. (1992) *Backlash: The Undeclared War Against Women*, London, Chatto & Windus.

Ferraro, K. (1981) 'Processing Battered Women', *Journal of Family Issues*, vol. 2, no. 4, pp. 425–38.

Ferraro, K. (1983) 'Negotiating Trouble in a Battered Women's Shelter', *Urban Life*, vol. 12, no. 3, pp. 287–306.

Finkelhor, D. (1984) *Child Sexual Abuse: New Theory and Research*, London, Free Press, Collier-Macmillan.

Finkelhor, D. (1986) *A Sourcebook on Child Sexual Abuse*, New York, Sage.

Foley, M. (1991) 'Rape: A Feminist Analysis of Recent Public Service Provisions for Women with Particular Reference to the Sexual Assault Referral Centre', unpublished Ph. D. thesis.

Freidson, E. (1970) *Professional Dominance, the Social Structure of Medical Care*, New York, Aldine Publishing Company.

French, M. (1986) *Beyond Power: On Women, Men and Morals*, London, Abacus.

Frost, N. and Stein, M. (1989) *The Politics of Child Welfare: Inequalities, Power and Change*, Hemel Hempstead.

Furniss, T. (1991) *The Multi-Professional Handbook of Child Sexual Abuse*, London, Routledge.

Geraghty, J. (1991) *Probation Practice in Crime Prevention*, Paper 24, London, HMSO.

Gifford, Z. (1990) *The Golden Thread – Asian Experiences of Post-Raj Britain*, London, Grafton Books.

Gill, M. L. and Mawby, R. I. (1990) *Volunteers in the Criminal Justice System: A Comparative Study of Probation, Police and Victim Support*, Milton Keynes, Open University Press.

Glaser, D. and Frosh, S. (1988) *Child Sexual Abuse*, Basingstoke, Macmillan.

Glendinning, C. (1987) 'Impoverishing Women', in A. Walker and C. Walker (eds), *The Growing Divide*, London, Child Poverty Action Group.

Golding, R. (1992) 'Policing Prostitution', *Police Review*, vol. 8, Spring.

Goode, W. J. (1969) 'The Theoretical Limits of Professionalization', in A. Etzioni (ed.), *The Semi-Professions and their Ogranization*, New York, Free Press.

Greater Manchester Chief Constable's Report (1987).

Green, S. (1975) 'Professional/Bureaucratic Conflict: The NHS', *Sociological Review*, vol. 20, pp. 533–67.

Greer, G. (1971) *The Female Eunuch*, London, Paladin.

Hall, L. and Lloyd, S. (1989) *Surviving Child Sexual Abuse: a Handbook for Helping Women Challenge their Past*, London, Falmer Press.

Hammersley, M. and Atkinson, P. (1988) *Ethnography: Principles in Practice*, London, Tavistock Publications.

Hanmer, J. (1977) 'Community Action, Women's Aid and the Women's Liberation Movement', in M. Mayo (ed.), *Women in the Community*, London, Routledge & Kegan Paul.

Hanmer, J. (1978) 'Violence and the Social Control of Women', in C. Littlejohn (ed.), *Power and the State*, London, Croom Helm.

Hanmer, J. and Maynard, M. (1987) *Women, Violence and Social Control*, Basingstoke, Macmillan.

Hanmer, J. and Saunders S. (1984) *Well-founded Fear: A Community Study of Violence to Women*, London, Hutchinson.

Hanmer, J. and Statham, D. (1988) *Women and Social Work: Towards a Woman-Centred Practice*, Basingstoke, Macmillan.

Hanmer, J., Radford J., and Stanko, E. A. (eds), (1989) *Women, Policing and Male Violence: International Perspectives*, London, Routledge.

Harding, J. (ed.) (1987) *Probation in the Community: A Practice and Policy Reader*, London, Tavistock Publications.

Harper, J. (1991) 'What about the Wounded?', *Social Work Today*, 12 December.

Hatch, S. (1977) 'Voluntary Organisations – Some Research Priorities', in *Research into Voluntary Involvement*, London, Volunteer Society.

Heller, V. (1990) 'Sexual Liberalism and Survivors of Sexual Abuse', in D. Leidhort and J. G. Raymond (eds), *The Sexual Liberals and the Attack on Feminism*, New York, Pergamon Press.

Hester, M. (1992) *Lewd Women and Wicked Witches: A Study of the Dynamics of Male Domination*, London, Routledge.

Hester, M. and Florence, P. (1990) 'Gender Divisions and Violence in Social Work', paper presented to the British Sociological Annual Conference, University of Surrey.

HMSO (1987) *Violent Crime: Police Advice for Women on How to Reduce the Risks*, London, HMSO.

HMSO (1988) *Report of the Enquiry into Child Abuse in Cleveland*, London, HMSO.

HMSO (1989) *Caring for People: Community Care in the Next Decade and Beyond*, Cmnd. 849.

HMSO (1990) *Beating Crime*, London, HMSO.

HMSO (1991a) *British Crime Survey*, London, HMSO.

HMSO (1991b) *Working Together Under the Children Act, 1989*. A guide to arrangements for inter-agency co-operation for the protection of children from abuse, Home Office, Dept of Health, Dept of Education and Science and the Welsh Office, London, HMSO.

HMSO (1991c) *The Work of the Probation Service with Sex Offenders*, HM Inspectorate of Probation.

Hoff, A. L. and Williams, T. (1975) 'Counselling the Rape Victim and her Family', *Crisis Intervention*, vol. 6, no. 4, pp. 2–13.

Hoigard, C. and Finstad, L. (1992) *Backstreets: Prostitution, Money and Love*, Cambridge, Polity Press.

Home Office (1984) *Statement of National Objectives and Priorities for the Probation Service*.

Home Office (1990a) *Prison Statistics*, London, HMSO.

Home Office (1990b) *Crime, Justice and Protecting the Public*, Cmnd. 965, London, HMSO.

Home Office (1990c) *Victims' Charter*, London, HMSO.

Home Office (1990d) *Partnership in Dealing with Offenders in the Community*, London, HMSO.

Hooper, C. A. (1988) *Alternatives to Collusion: The Responses of Mothers to Child Sexual Abuse in the Family*, a paper presented to the Annual Conference of the British Psychological Society, University of Leeds.

Horley, S. (1988) *Love and Pain – A Survival Handbook for Women*, London, Bedford Square Press.

Horley, S. (1990a) 'Responding to Male Violence against Women', *NAPO Journal*, December.

Horley, S. (1990b) 'A Shame and a Disgrace', *Social Work Today*, 21 June.

Hudson, A. (1989) 'Changing Perspectives: Feminism, Gender and Social Work', in M. Langan, and P. Lee (eds), *Radical Social Work Today*, London, Unwin Hyman.

Hudson, A. (1992) 'The Child Sexual Abuse "Industry" and Gender Relations in Social Work', in M. Langan and L. Day (eds), *Women, Oppression and Social Work*, London, Routledge.

Hudson, D. (1987). 'You Can't Commit Violence Against an Object: Women, Psychiatry and Psychosurgery', in J. Hanmer and M. Maynard (eds), *Women, Violence and Social Control*, Basingstoke, Macmillan.

Humm, M. (ed.) (1992) *Feminisms: A Reader*, Hemel Hempstead, Harvester-Wheatsheaf.

Hunt Bagg, C. (1990) 'Terror in the Home – Domestic Violence in the Indian Community – How Serious Is It?', *India Currents*, vol. 4, no. 9, December, S. California.

Interdepartmental Group on Child Abuse (1992) *A Strategic Statement on Working with Abusers*.

Jackson, M. (1984). 'Sexology and the Social Construction of Male Sexuality', in L. Coveney *et al.* (eds), *The Sexuality Papers*, London, Hutchinson.

Jaget, C. (ed.) (1980) *Prostitutes Our Life*, Bristol, Falling Wall Press.

Jamdagni, L. (1980) 'Hamari Rangali Zindagi – Our Colourful lives', unpublished report.

James, D. (1990) *Domestic Violence and the Asian Community in Hounslow*, London Borough of Hounslow.

Jansari, A. (1980) 'Social Work with Ethnic Minorities – A Review of Literature', *Multi-Racial Social Work*, no. VI, p. 17.

Jeffreys, S. (1990) *Anticlimax*, London, Women's Press.

Johnson, J. M. (1981) 'Program Enterprise and Official Cooptation in the Battered Women's Shelter Movement', *American Behavioral Scientist*, vol. 29, no. 6, pp. 827–42.

Johnson, S. (1988) 'Guidelines for Social Workers in Coping with Violent Clients', *British Journal of Social Work*, no. 18, 377–90.

Jones, A. (1991) *Women Who Kill*, London, Gollancz.

Jones, C. (1989) 'The End of the Road? Issues in Social Work Education', in P. Carter *et al.* (eds), *Social Work and Social Welfare Yearbook, 1*, Milton Keynes, Open University Press.

Jowell, R. and Airey, C. (1984) *British Social Attitudes*, London, Gower.

Judkins, B. M. (1989) 'The Black Lung Movement: Social Movements and Social Structure', in L. Kriesberg (ed.), *Research on Social Movements, Conflict and Change*, Greenwich, JAI.

Jukes, A. (1990) 'Making Women Safe', *Community Care*, vol. 21, no. 41.

Kaplan, H. S. (1974) *The New Sex Therapy*, London, Baillière Tindall.

Katz, S. (1979) *Understanding the Rape Victim*, New York, John Wiley.

Kelly, L. (1988) *Surviving Sexual Violence*, Cambridge, Polity Press.

Kelly, L. (1989a) 'The Professionalization of Rape', *Rights of Women Bulletin*, Spring, pp. 8–11.

Kelly, L. (1989b) 'Bitter Ironies: The Professionalisation of Child Abuse', *Trouble and Strife*, vol. 16, pp. 14–21.

Kelly, L. (1991) 'Women's Refuges: 20 Years On', *Spare Rib*, no. 221, pp. 32–5.

Kelly, L. and Radford, J. (1987) 'The Problem of Men: Feminist Perspectives on Sexual Violence', in P. Scraton (ed.), *Law, Order and the Authoritarian State*, Milton Keynes, Open University Press.

Kelly, L., Regan, L. and Burton, S. (1991) *An Exploratory Study of the Prevalence of Sexual Abuse in a Sample of 16–21 Year Olds*, Child Abuse Studies Unit, University of North London.

King, J. (1989) 'How Do You Handle Violence?', *Community Care*, no. 755, pp. 23–4.

Koss, M. P. and Harvey, M. R. (1991) *The Rape Victim*, London, Sage Publications.

Langan, M. and Day, L. (eds) (1992) *Women, Oppression and Social Work*, London, Routledge.

Langan, M. and Lee, P. (1989) *Radical Social Work*, London, Unwin Hyman.

Lash, S. (1992) *Restructuring and the Underclass: European versus American Variants*, paper given to the annual conference of the British Sociological Association, 6–9 April 1992, Canterbury, University of Kent.

Leonard, P. and McLeod, E. (1980) *Marital Violence: Social Construction and Social Service Response*, Warwick, Department of Applied Social Studies.

Levitas, R. (1983) 'Feminism and Human Nature', in I. Forbes and S. Smith (eds), *Politics and Human Nature*, London, Pinter.

Locke, T. (1990) *New Approaches to Crime in the 1990s*, London, Longman.

London Rape Crisis Centre (1984) *Sexual Violence: The Reality for Women*, London, Women's Press.

Lorenz, K. (1966) *On Aggression*, London, Macmillan.

Lovell, T. (ed.) (1990) *British Feminist Thought: A Reader*, Oxford, Basil Blackwell.

Luckhaus, L. (1985) 'A Plea for PMT in the Criminal Law', in S. Edwards (ed.), *Gender, Sex and the Law*, Beckenham, Croom Helm.

Maccoby, E. and Jacklin, C. N. (1974) *The Psychology of Sex Differences*, Oxford, Oxford University Press.

MacKinnon, C. (1979) *Sexual Harassment of Working Women*, Harvard, Harvard University Press.

MacLeod, M. and Saraga, E. (1988a) *Child Sexual Abuse: Towards a Feminist Professional Practice*, Report of a Conference held at the Polytechnic of North London.

MacLeod, M. and Saraga, E. (1988b) 'Challenging the Orthodoxy: Towards a Feminist Theory and Practice', in *Family Secrets: Child Sexual Abuse, Feminist Review*, no. 28, January, pp. 16–55.

MacVaugh, G. S. (1979). *Frigidity – What You Should Know about its Cure with Hypnosis*, Oxford, Pergamon Press.

Maguire, M. and Pointing, J. (eds) (1988) *Victims of Crime: A New Deal?*, Milton Keynes, Open University Press.

Maguire, S. (1988) 'Sorry Love' – Violence in the Home and the State Response', *Critical Social Policy*, 23, vol. 8 (2), pp. 34–45.

Mahony, P. (1985) *Schools for the Boys?*, London, Hutchinson.

Mama, A. (1989a) 'Violence against Black Women – Gender, Race and State Responses', *Feminist Review*, no. 32, p. 31.

Mama, A. (1989b) *The Hidden Struggle – statutory and voluntary sector responses to violence against black women in the home*, London, Race and Housing Research Unit.

Masson, H. and O'Byrne, P. (1990) 'The Family Systems Approach: A Help or Hindrance?', in Violence Against Children Study Group, *Taking Child Abuse Seriously: Contemporary Issues in Child Protection Theory and Practice*, London, Unwin Hyman.

Matthews, R. (1986) 'Beyond Wolfenden? Prostitution, Politics and the Law', in R. Matthews and J. Young (eds), *Confronting Crime*, London, Sage Publications.

Mawby, R. I and Gill, M. L. (1987) *Crime Victims: Needs, Services and the Voluntary Sector*, London, Tavistock.

Maynard M. (1993) 'Violence towards Women', in D. Richardson and V. Robinson (eds), *Introducing Women's Studies*, Basingstoke, Macmillan.

Maynard, M. (1985) 'The Response of Social Workers to Domestic Violence', in J. Pahl (ed.), *Private Violence and Public Policy*, London, Routledge & Kegan Paul.

McKinlay, J. B. (1973) 'On the Professional Regulation of Change', in P. Halmos (ed.), *Professionalization and Social Change*, Sociological Review Monograph no. 20, University of Keele.

McNay, M. (1992) 'Social Work and Power Relations: Towards a Framework for Integrated Practice', in M. Langan and L. Day (eds), *Women, Oppression and Social Work*, London, Routledge.

McNeill, S. (1985) 'In Steering Women who have been Raped to Sex Therapists We are Performing a Function to Men, and Gluing over a Crack in Male Supremacy', in D. Rhodes and S. McNeill (eds), *Women Against Violence Against Women*, London, Only Women Press.

Meadows, A. (1975) *In Search of Identity*, London, YWCA.

Middleton, J. (1991) 'Marrying for Money', *Young People Now*, no. 27, July, Leicester, National Youth Agency.

Miller, A. (1987) *For Your Own Good: The Roots of Violence in Child Rearing*, London, Virago.

Miller, A. C. (1990) 'The Mother–Daughter Relationship and the Distortion of Reality in Childhood Sexual Abuse', in R. J. Perelberg and A. C. Miller (eds), *Gender and Power in Families*, London, Routledge.

Moore, J. (1990) 'Confronting the Perpetrator', *Community Care*, 12 April.

Morgan, D. (1987) 'Masculinity and Violence' in J. Hanmer and M. Maynard (eds), *Women, Violence and Social Control*, Basingstoke, Macmillan.

Morgan, P. A. (1985) 'Constructing Images of Deviance: A Look at State Intervention into the Problem of Wife Beating', in N. Johnson (ed.) *Marital Violence*, London, Routledge & Kegan Paul.

Murray, S. B. (1988) 'The Unhappy Marriage of Theory and Practice: An Analysis of a Battered Women's Shelter', *National Women's Studies Association Journal*, vol. 11, pp. 75–92.

NAPO (1990) 'Working with Women: An Anti-Sexist Approach', Probation Practice Committee Paper, July, pp. 41–90.

NAVSS (1986) *Training Manual for Supporting Female Victims of Sexual Assault*, London, NAVSS.

Nelson, S. (1987) *Incest: Fact and Myth*, Stramullion Co-operative Ltd.

NPRIE (1990) *Index of Probation Projects*, National Probation Research and Information Exchange.

O'Hagan, K. (1989) 'Split Decisions Prevent Progress', *Community Care*, 9 March, p. 13.

O'Hagan, K. (1989) *Working with Child Sex Abuse*, Milton Keynes, Open University Press.

O'Neill, M. (1991a) *Prostitution, Ideology and the Structuration of Gender Relations: Towards a Critical Feminist Praxis*, paper given to the annual British Sociological Association conference, University of Kent, Canterbury, 6–9 April 1992.

O'Neill, M. (1991b) *Prostitution in Nottingham: Towards a Multi-Agency Approach*, Nottingham Polytechnic.

O'Neill, M. (1992a) 'Women at Work: Prostitution in the Context of Late Modernity', *Phoebe: An International Journal of Feminist Scholarship, Theory and Aesthetics*, vol. 4 no. 1, SUNY, Spring.

O'Neill, M. (1992b) *Academic Power and Social Knowledge: Prostitution, Critical Theory and Feminist Praxis*, conference paper forthcoming in Brown, Weeks and Schumway (eds), *Academic Knowledge and Social Power*, University of Virginia Press. This collection is a result of the international conference organised by Richard Brown, University of Maryland, College Park, 20–22 November 1992.

O'Neill, M. (1992c) 'Prostitution in Nottingham', *Nottingham Justices' Journal*, no. 15, February.

O'Sullivan, E. (1978) 'What Has Happened to Rape Crisis Centres? A Look at Their Structures, Members and Funding', *Victimology: an International Journal*, vol. 3, nos 1–2, pp. 45–62.

Offe, C. (1984) *Contradictions of the Welfare State*, London, Hutchinson.

Open University (1983) *What is Discrimination? Racism in the Workplace and Community*, Milton Keynes, Open University Press.

Pahl, J. (1979) 'Refuges for Battered Women: Social Provision or Social Movement?, *Journal of Voluntary Action Research*, vol. 8, nos 1–2, pp. 25–35.

Pahl, J. (1985a) *Private Violence and Public Policy*, London, Routledge & Kegan Paul.

Pahl, J. (1985b) 'Refuges for Battered Women: Ideology and Action', *Feminist Review*, vol. 19, pp. 25–43.

Parmar, P. (1982) *The Empire Strikes Back – Racism in 70s Britain*, Centre for Contemporary Cultural Studies, University of Birmingham, London, Hutchinson.

Parole Board (1991) *Report of the Parole Board for 1990*, London, HMSO.

Parsloe, P. (1989) 'The Future of Social Work Education: Recovering from Care Tomorrow', in P. Carter *et al.*, *Social Work and Social Welfare Yearbook, 1*, Milton Keynes, Open University Press.

Parton, C. (1990) 'Women, Gender Oppression and Child Abuse', in *Taking Child Abuse Seriously*, Violence Against Children Study Group, London, Unwin Hyman.

Percival, L. (1989) 'Confronting Gender Issues', *Community Care*, 23 November.

Pheonix, A. (1990) 'Theories of Gender and Black Families', in Lovell, T. (ed.), *British Feminist Thought: A Reader*, Oxford, Basil Blackwell.

Pheterson, G. (1986) *The Whore Stigma*, sponsored by the Dutch Ministry.

204   *References*

Pheterson, G. (1990) 'The Category "Prostitute" in Scientific Enquiry', *Journal of Sex Research*, vol. 27, no. 3, August, pp. 397–407.

Pheterson, G. (ed.) (1989) *A Vindication of the Rights of Whores*, Washington, Seal Press.

Pizzey, E. (1974) *Scream Quietly or the Neighbours Will Hear*, Harmondsworth, Penguin.

Price, L. (1988) 'In Women's Interests: Feminist Activism and Institutional Change', *Women's Research Centre Report*, Vancouver.

Pride, A. (1991) 'To Respectability and Back: A Ten-Year View of the Anti-Rape Movement', in F. Delacoste and F. Newman (eds), *Fight Back! Feminist Resistance to Male Violence*, Pittsburgh, Cleiss Press.

Priorities for the Probation Service, Cmnd. 963, London, HMSO.

Radford, J. (1989) 'Police Response to Rape', *Rights of Women Bulletin*, Spring, pp. 6–8.

Ramazanoglu, C. (1989) *Feminism and the Contradictions of Oppression*, London, Routledge.

Redding, D. (1991) 'Voluntary Severance', *Community Care*, 25 April, p. 7.

Renvoize, J. (1982) *Incest: A Family Pattern*, London, Routledge & Kegan Paul.

Rivera, A. (1989) 'Working with Mothers of Sexually-Abused Children', ISO-SAC (In Support Of Sexually Abused Children).

Roberts, R. (1984) 'The Case for a Sexual Assault Referral Centre in Manchester', unpublished paper.

Robins, D. (1984) *We Hate Humans*, Harmondsworth, Penguin.

Rock, P. (1988) 'Government, Victims and Policies in Two Countries', *British Journal of Criminology*, vol. 28, no. 1, pp. 44–66.

Rock, P. (1990) *Helping Victims of Crime: The Home Office and the Rise of Victim Support in England and Wales*, Oxford, Clarendon Press.

Roehl, J. E. and Gray, D. (1984) 'The Crisis of Rape: A Guide to Counselling Victims of Rape', *Crisis Intervention*, vol. 13, no. 2, pp. 67–77.

Rose, H. (1985) 'Women's Refuges: Erecting New Forms of Welfare?', in C. Ungerson (ed.), *Women and Social Policy*, London, Macmillan.

Rowett, C. (1986) *Violence in Social Work*, Cambridge, Cambridge University Institute of Criminology.

RTI (1991) *Funding Digest*, Newcastle upon Tyne, Research Training Initiatives.

Rush, F. (1990) 'The Many Faces of Backlash', in D. Leidholdt and J.G. Raymond (eds), *The Sexual Liberals and the Attack on Feminism*, Oxford, Pergamon Press.

Russell, D.E.H. (1984) *Sexual Exploitation*, London, Sage Publications.

Russell, D.E.H. (1986) *The Secret Trauma: Incest in the Lives of Girls and Women*, New York, Basic Books.

Ryan, W. (1971) *Blaming the Victim*, New York, Pantheon Books.

SARC Progress Report (1988) and (1991), Manchester.

Saunders, D.G. (1988) 'Wife Abuse, Husband Abuse or Mutual Combat?', in K. Yllo and M. Bograd (eds), *Feminist Perspectives in Wife Abuse*, London, Sage Publications.

Saunders, L. (1987) 'Safe and Secure in Surrey?', *Social Services Research*, nos 5/6, pp. 32–55.

Sayers, J. (1986) *Sexual Contradictions*, London, Tavistock Publications.

Schechter, S. (1981) 'The Future of the Battered Women's Movement', in F. Delacoste and F. Newman (eds), *Fight Back! Feminist Resistance to Male Violence*, London, Routledge & Kegan Paul.

Schechter, S. (1982) *Women and Male Violence: The Visions and Struggles of the Battered Women's Movement*, London, Pluto Press.

Schultz, L.G. (1987) 'The Social Worker as Victim of Violence', *Social Casework*, no. 68, pp. 240–4.

Scott, S. and Dickens, A. (1989) 'Police and the Professionalization of Rape', in C. Dunhill (ed.) *The Boys in Blue*, London, Virago.

Scottish Women's Aid (1991), *Change* Annual Report.

Scottish Women's Aid (n.d.) *Working with Asian Women*, Edinburgh, Scottish Women's Aid.

Scully, D. (1990) *Understanding Sexual Violence*, London, Unwin Hyman.

Segal, L. (1987) *Is the Future Female*? London, Virago.

Segal, L. (1991) *Slow Motion*, London, Virago.

Shan, S. (1985) *In My Own Name*, London, The Women's Press Ltd.

Shapland, J. *et al.* (1985) *Victims in the Criminal Justice System*, Aldershot, Gower.

Shardlow, S. (1989) *The Value of Change in Social Work*, London, Tavistock/Routledge.

Sharpe, S. (1976) *Just Like a Girl*, Harmondsworth, Penguin.

Sharron, H. (1981) 'The Souring of the Partnership', *Voluntary Action*, NCVO, Winter, pp. 18–20.

Sharron, H. (1985) 'When Terror Is a Fact of Life', *Social Work Today*, vol. 17, no. i, pp. 8–9.

Sitaram, S. (1985) 'Ethnic Minority Communities in Southampton', unpublished paper.

Small, N. (1987) 'Putting Violence to Social Workers into Context', *Critical Social Policy*, no. 9, pp. 40–51.

Smart, C. (1985) 'Legal Subjects and Sexual Objects', in J. Brophy and C. Smart (eds), *Women in Law: Explorations in Law, Family and Sexuality*, London, Routledge.

Smith, V. (1990) 'Split Affinities', in M. Hirsch and E. Keller (eds), *Conflicts in Feminism*, London, Routledge.

Southall Black Sisters (n.d.) *Domestic Violence: There Is Something You Can Do*, London, Ealing Council's Women's Unit.

Spare Rib (1990) no. 214, July.

Srinivasan, M. and Davis, L. V. (1991) 'A Shelter: An Organisation Like Any Other?', *Affilia*, vol. 6, no. 1, pp. 38–57.

Stanko, E. (1989) 'Missing the Mark? Policing Battering', in J. Hanmer *et al.* (eds), *Women, Policing and Male Violence*, London, Routledge.

Stanko, E. (1990) *Everyday Violence*, London, Pandora Press.

Stanko, E. A. (1985) *Intimate Intrusions? Women's Experiences of Male Violence*, London, Routledge & Kegan Paul.

Stanley, L. (ed.) (1990) *Feminist Praxis: Research, Theory and Epistemology in Feminist Sociology*, London, Routledge.

Stevenson, P. (1989) 'Women in Special Hospitals', *Open Mind*, no. 41, October/November.

Storr, A. (1964) *Sexual Deviation*, Harmondsworth, Penguin.

Storr, A. (1968) *Human Aggression*, Harmondsworth, Penguin.

Straus, M. A. *et al.* (1980) 'Victims and Aggressors in Marital Violence', *American Behavioral Scientist*, vol. 23, no. 5, pp. 618–704.

Swarup, N. (1992) *Equal Voice: The Service Needs of Black Communities*, Social Services Research and Information Unit, Report no. 22, University of Portsmouth.

Tang Nain, G. (1991) 'Black Women, Sexism and Racism – Black or Anti-Racist Feminism', *Feminist Review*, no. 37, p. 1.

Thornton, P. (1991) 'Once More Unto the Breach', *Social Work Today*, vol. 22, no. 43, p. 21.

Tice, K. W. (1990) 'A Case Study of Battered Women's Shelters in Appalachia', *Affilia*, vol. 5, no. 3, pp. 83–100.

Tierney, K. (1982) 'The Battered Women Movement and the Creation of the Wife Beating Problem', *Social Problems*, vol. 29, no. 3, 206–20.

Toner, B. (1982) *The Facts of Rape*, revised edn, London, Arrow.

Tong, R. (1989) *Feminist Thought: A Comprehensive Introduction*, London, Routledge.

Toronto Rape Crisis (1985) 'Rape', in C. Guberman and M. Wolfe (eds), *No Safe Place: Violence Against Women and Children*, Canada, Women's Press.

Turner, B. (1987) *Medical Power and Social Knowledge*, London, Sage Publications.

Turner, J. (1989) *Home Is Where the Hurt Is*, Wellingborough, Thorson.

Viinnikka, S.(1989) 'Child Sexual Abuse and the Law', in E. Driver and A. Droisen (eds), *Child Sexual Abuse: Feminist Perspectives*, Basingstoke, Macmillan.

Walby, S. (1990) *Theorizing Patriarchy*, Oxford, Basil Blackwell.

Walklate, S. (1989) *Victimology: The Victim and the Criminal Justice Process*, London, Unwin Hyman.

Watson, L. and Cooper, R. (1991) *A Study of Special Needs Housing Provided by Housing Associations – First Stage Report*, Department of Sociology and Social Policy, University of Southampton.

Westwood, S. (1984) *All Day Every Day – Factory and Family in the Making of Women's Lives*, London, Pluto Press.

Wharton, S.C. (1987) 'Establishing Shelters for Battered Women: Local Manifestation of a Social Problem', *Qualitative Sociology*, 10, pp. 146–63.

White, E. (1986a) *Chain Chain Change – for Black Women Dealing with Physical and Emotional Abuse*, Seattle, Seal Press.

White, T. (1986b) 'Progress Report on the Proposed Sexual Assault Centre', 7 May.

Whitehouse, P.(1986) 'Race and the Criminal Justice System', in V. Coombe and A. Little (eds), *Race and Social Work*, London, Tavistock Publications.

Williams, G. (1983) *Inner City Policy: A Partnership with the Voluntary Sector?*, NCVO Occasional Paper, London, Bedford Square Press.

Wilson, E. (1983) *What Is to be Done about Violence against Women – Crisis in the Eighties*, Harmondsworth, Penguin.

Wise, S. (1985) 'Becoming a Feminist Social Worker', *Studies in Sexual Politics*, Department of Sociology, University of Manchester.

Wistow, G. *et al.* (1992) 'From Providing to Enabling: Local Authorities and the Mixed Economy of Care', *Public Administration*, vol. 70, Spring, pp. 25–45.

Wolmar, C. (1988) 'Refuge Rule Change Shuts Out Women', *Observer*, 2 October.

Woolf, V. (1977) *Three Guineas* (first published 1938), Harmondsworth, Penguin.

Worral, A. (1990) *Offending Women*, London, Routledge.

Wyre, R. (1986) *Women, Men and Rape*, Oxford, Perry Publications.

Yllo, K. and Bograd, M. (eds) (1988) *Feminist Perspectives on Wife Abuse*, London, Sage.

Notes on Contributors

Claudia Bernard is a Senior Lecturer in Social Work at the University of Portsmouth. Prior to that she worked for a number of years in local authority as a generic social worker. Her research interests are broad-ranging but include a focus on the relationship between race, gender, social class and social welfare.

Kish Bhatti-Sinclair has been working alternatively within the voluntary sector and higher education for thirteen years. She is a qualified youth and community worker and currently teaches in the Department of Social Work Studies at the University of Southampton. Her main interests lie in the area of equal opportunities, anti-racist social work, young people, housing, and computers in higher education. She is an active member of her local Asian Women Against Violence and Abuse Group.

Marian Foley has been actively involved in rape crisis work for the last eight years. Her doctoral research was on the establishment and operation of the Manchester Sexual Assault Referral Centre. Her future research interests are in the work of sexual assault centres in other countries and in the experience of women in prison who have experienced men's sexual violence.

Terry Gillespie is a Lecturer in Sociology at Nottingham Trent University and is course leader of the BA Criminology Course in the Department of Applied Social Studies. Terry was a volunteer with a rape crisis centre for five years and her current research critically examines changing organisational modes within rape crisis centres in the context of the growth of service provision both by the police and victim support schemes.

Marianne Hester is a Lecturer in Social Studies (Continuing Education) at the University of Exeter. She has carried out research into many aspects of violence against women and has been involved in action around violence and work with survivors at the same time. Her publications include *Lewd Women and Wicked Witches: A Study of the Dynamics of Male Domination*.

209

Carol Lupton is Head of the Social Services Research and Information Unit (SSRIU) at the University of Portsmouth. Her main research interests are in the area of the organisation and delivery of health and social care services. Carol was a founding member of Portsmouth Women's Aid and served for many years on the Refuge Support Group.

Maggie O'Neill is a Lecturer in Sociology and Assistant Director of the Crime Reduction Research Unit at Nottingham Trent University. She has been engaged in feminist research on prostitution since 1990 and is a founder member of the East Midlands Forum into Prostitution. Maggie is currently researching both routes into prostitution from local authority care and, with POW (Prostitute Outreach Workers), exit routes for women who want to leave prostitution.

Joan Orme is a Senior Lecturer and Head of Department Elect in the Department of Social Work Studies at the University of Southampton. Her background is in the probation service. Joan's publications include books on workload management issues: *Managing People in the Personal Social Services* (with Bryan Glastonbury and Richard Bradley), and *Care Management: Tasks and Workloads* (with Bryan Glastonbury).

Stella Perrott joined the probation service in 1979 and has worked in field and prison teams. She spent three years working with female prisoners in Durham 'H' Wing (many of whom had been abused by men, both as children and as adults), while at the same time working with male abusers in the main part of the prison. She is currently an Assistant Chief Probation Officer and has been an active member of the National Association of Probation Officers and also Women in NAPO (WIN).

Index